BEGINNING ACOUSTIC GUITAR

The Complete Acoustic Guitar Method

Beginning · Intermediate · Mastering

GREG HORNE

Alfred, the leader in educational publishing, and the National Guitar Workshop, one of America's finest guitar schools, have joined forces to bring you the best, most progressive educational tools possible. We hope you will enjoy this book and encourage you to look for other fine products from Alfred and the National Guitar Workshop.

ISBN 0-7390-0423-9 Book
ISBN 0-7390-0424-7 Book & CD
ISBN 0-7390-3763-3 Book & DVD

This book was acquired, edited and produced
by Workshop Arts, Inc., the publishing arm of the National Guitar Workshop.

Nathaniel Gunod, editor
Joe Bouchard, music typesetter
Timothy Phelps, interior book design
The CD was recorded at Bar None Studios, Cheshire, CT

Cover photographs (clockwise from upper left:) Photodisc; Karen Miller; Jeff Oshiro; Planet Art;
(series) Karen Miller /Ted Engelbart, Greg McKinney, Photodisc.

TABLE OF CONTENTS

ABOUT THE AUTHOR

PHOTO • STUART RABINOWITZ

Greg Horne is a performer, writer, producer and teacher. He holds a Bachelor of Arts in Music from the College of Wooster, and pursued graduate studies at the University of Mississippi's Center for the Study of Southern Culture. Greg has been an instructor at the National Guitar Workshop's summer campuses since 1990, specializing in acoustic and blues courses. He also teaches privately. In 1998, he produced an album of original songs entitled "Floating World." Greg has produced albums for singer-songwriters Deirdre Flint and Jodie Manross. He lives in Knoxville, Tennessee, where he fronts a rock'n'roll band, plays old-time fiddle and writes songs.

00

Track
01

A compact disc is available with each book of this series. Using these discs will help make learning more enjoyable and the information more meaningful. The CD will help you play the correct notes, rhythms and feel of each example. The track numbers below the symbols correspond directly to the example you want to hear. Track I will help you tune to this CD. Have fun!

INTRODUCTION

Welcome to *The Complete Acoustic Guitar Method,* a comprehensive series of books designed specifically for the modern acoustic guitarist. Each of the three volumes incorporates rhythm playing, soloing, easy-to-understand music theory and exciting techniques.

Beginning Acoustic Guitar is designed for the beginning guitarist. By the time you complete this book, you will be able to do the following:

1. Read music in the first position.
2. Play all of the major and minor open chords.
3. Play a variety of strums that sound great for folk, rock and bluegrass styles.
4. Play the two most popular barre chord forms.
5. Play a blues chord progression and improvise a blues solo.
6. Fingerpick in basic arpeggio and alternating bass patterns.

HOW TO USE THIS BOOK:

The individual lessons in this book are grouped by subject into chapters. Once you have covered the basic material in Chapter 1, you can skip around to different chapters in the book. Each chapter is progressive, meaning each lesson builds on the previous ones in that chapter. You may want to work your way through a couple of chapters at a time, alternating lessons for variety.

WHERE TO GO FROM HERE:

This book will give you the foundation of skills needed to study any style of guitar. You can continue in this series, or use this volume to get you ready for other National Guitar Workshop/Alfred methods. Here are some suggestions, depending on your personal goals.

IF YOUR GOAL IS...
To be able to play chords, melodies and solos for group singing, songwriting, or jamming with others...
THEN TRY... *Beginning Acoustic Guitar,* which will give you the skills you need! Also try *Folk Guitar for Beginners* and the *Acoustic Rock Stand Alone* CD.

IF YOUR GOAL IS...
To learn more about the techniques heard in modern acoustic music—including rock, funk, blues, bluegrass and Celtic styles; to learn to improvise in a variety of scales and play in alternate tunings...
THEN TRY... *Intermediate Acoustic Guitar* and *Mastering Acoustic Guitar.*

IF YOUR GOAL IS...
To learn more about rock, jazz, or blues improvisation and chords...
THEN TRY... *The Complete Rock Guitar Method, The Complete Jazz Guitar Method* and/or *The Complete Blues Guitar Method* and some of the 20 different *Stand Alone* play-along CDs.

To learn more about fingerstyle guitar after *Beginning Acoustic Guitar,* check out *The Complete Fingerstyle Guitar Method.*

This volume is dedicated to my family and my music teachers. Special thanks to Lou Manzi, David Smolover, Nat Gunod, Jody Fisher and Seth Austen.

CHAPTER 1

Getting Started

This chapter is a review of basic materials. If you already read music and tablature, know how to find any note on the guitar, know some basic chords (such as D, A, G, E and C) and are familiar with basic technique, you can skip this chapter and begin with Chapter 2 which begins on page 16. But before you do, thumb through this chapter and make sure you understand all the material.

LESSON 1: GETTING TO KNOW YOUR TOOLS

TIPS FOR LEFTIES

This series of books is oriented toward right-handed guitar playing. Many left-handed players play guitar right-handed. Others can simply reverse the instructions found in this series.

THE PARTS OF THE GUITAR

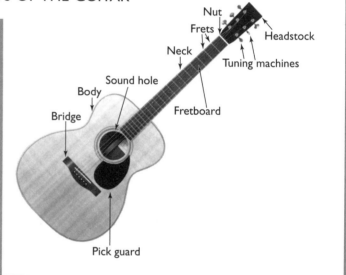

THE NATURAL CURVE

The shoulders, arms, hands and fingers all function best in a relaxed position. Hold your wrist and fingers in a loosely curled position. Any time you flex your wrist or fingers against their natural curve, you put a strain on the ligaments and tendons that control your fingers. This can result in pain and injury.

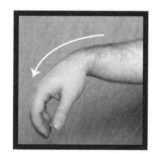

HOLDING THE GUITAR

There are several ways to hold the guitar. They are all governed by the same principle: *relax and follow the natural curves of the body.* Place your guitar so that your back is straight and your hands have easy access to the guitar without stretching or straining. The photos below show some commonly used positions:

Classical

Folk

Standing

THE LEFT-HAND POSITION

Your left hand should follow a gentle curve through the wrist and fingers. Place your thumb behind the neck, parallel to the frets. Touch the guitar with the pad of your thumb and your fingertips only. Keep your wrist slightly curved and your hand open, as if there was an imaginary golf ball in your palm.

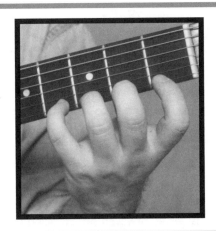

Finger Numbers

Your left-hand fingers are numbered as follows:

Index	=	1st Finger
Middle	=	2nd Finger
Ring	=	3rd Finger
Pinky	=	4th Finger

FRETTING NOTES

To fret a note, press your finger just to the left of the fret you want to play. Do not play on top of the fret. We often think in terms of *position*. A position is one finger per fret over a four-fret span. A position is defined by which fret your 1st finger is on. For example, in 1st position, your 1st finger plays the 1st fret. In 10th position, your 1st finger plays the 10th fret.

THE PICK

Most of this book is oriented toward playing with a *pick* (also known as a *flatpick* or *plectrum*). These are available in a wide variety of shapes and sizes. As you begin, try using a standard, teardrop-shaped pick in a medium or heavy gauge. These allow a great deal of control and more tone from the guitar than the thinner picks. Later, you may want to experiment with different picks. This book may also be studied with the use of a *thumbpick* (see the Appendix on page 92).

Top

Actual size

Point

HOLDING THE PICK

Place your right-hand thumb across the top of the pick, with the point at a 90-degree angle from your thumb. Then, curve your index finger behind the pick of the pick, holding it between your thumb and the side of the first joint of your index finger. Your other fingers can curl into your palm or hang loosely. Just keep them relaxed.

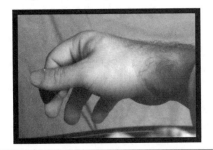

TUNING

The strings can be tuned to a piano, a tuner or to themselves. To tune to a piano, match the strings to the keys as shown. To tune the strings to each other, follow Steps 1 through 6 shown on the right. Play an open string, then play the matching note on the next lower string. Tune the open string up or down until the notes match exactly. Tuning takes practice, and you may want to enlist the help of an experienced player. See page 93 for more information about tuning. When tuning the guitar to itself, start from the lowest sounding strings and work up to the highest.

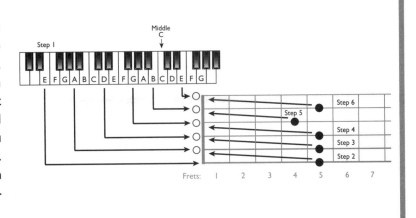

LESSON 2: THE NOTES ON THE FRETBOARD

The trick to learning the notes on the fingerboard is understanding the musical alphabet. This is easy. You only need to remember four things:

1. **The musical alphabet goes from A to G, then starts over again with A:**

   > A B C D E F G A B C and so on

   This series of seven notes, called *natural notes*, repeats in a continuous cycle.

2. **The shortest distance between two notes is a half step.**

   The closest one note can be to another is the distance of one fret. The distance between two notes that are on adjacent frets is called a *half step*. For example, from the 1st fret to the 2nd fret is a half step. The distance of two frets is called a *whole step*. For example, from the 1st fret to the 3rd fret is a whole step.

   > Half step   =   One Fret
   > Whole step   =   Two Frets

3. **In the musical alphabet, two sets of notes are only one half step apart.**

   > B to C is a half step
   > E to F is a half step

   There is no note between B and C, or between E and F. All the other natural notes are separated by one whole step.

4. **Special symbols called *accidentals* are used to name the notes between the natural notes.** Remember, there are no notes between E and F, or B and C.

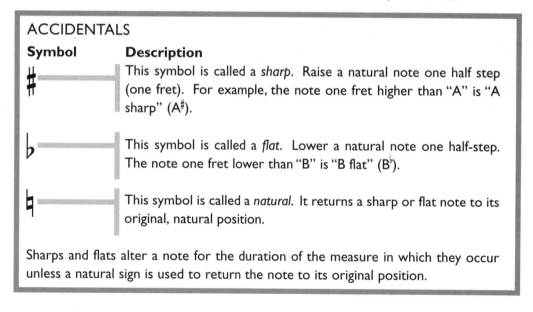

ACCIDENTALS

Symbol	Description
♯	This symbol is called a *sharp*. Raise a natural note one half step (one fret). For example, the note one fret higher than "A" is "A sharp" (A♯).
♭	This symbol is called a *flat*. Lower a natural note one half-step. The note one fret lower than "B" is "B flat" (B♭).
♮	This symbol is called a *natural*. It returns a sharp or flat note to its original, natural position.

Sharps and flats alter a note for the duration of the measure in which they occur unless a natural sign is used to return the note to its original position.

All sharp notes can have a flat name, and all flat notes can have a sharp name. For example, A♯ and B♭ fall on the same fret. Two notes that have different names but have the same sound are called *enharmonic equivalents*.

POP QUIZ:

What is the pitch between A and B called?   _A sharp (A♯) or B flat (B♭)_

What is the pitch between C and D called?   _____

Fill in the note names:

A ___ A♯B♭ ___ B ___ C ___ ___ D ___ ___ E ___ F ___ ___ G ___ ___
    Example

Check your answers by looking at the 5th string on the chart at the bottom of this page.

Practice saying the music alphabet forward and backward. Remember that as you go forward through the alphabet, the notes get higher in pitch. As you go backward, the notes get lower in pitch.

THE STRINGS

Your strings are tuned to the following pitches, low string to high:

Note:	E	A	D	G	B	E
String:	6	5	4	3	2	1

One fun way to remember this is to use the first letter of each word in this sentence:

Eat **A**t **D**ave's, **G**et **B**etter **E**ggs

Start on any open string and follow the alphabet series up the neck. Check your answers on the chart at the bottom of the page.

For example: Going up the 6th or 1st (E) string (either one):

Open	= E	7th fret =
1st fret	= F	8th fret =
2nd fret	= F♯ or G♭	9th fret =
3rd fret	= G	10th fret =
4th fret	= G♯ or A♭	11th fret =
5th fret	=	12th fret =
6th fret	=	

NOTE:

Notice that the 12th fret brings you back to where you started. You have gone an *octave* (distance of twelve half steps)—one cycle through the alphabet! This is why we say the guitar neck "starts over" at the 12th fret.

Here are all the notes on the guitar neck from the open string to the 12th fret:

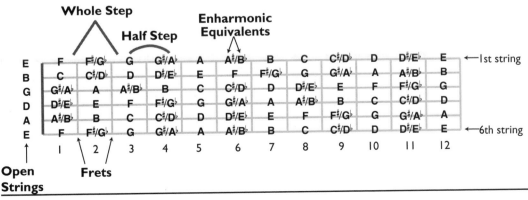

Now that we've covered the basics, it's time to play a few melodies.

TABLATURE

Tablature, called *TAB* for short, is a system of writing music just for the guitar. It tells you what fret to play and what string to play it on.

When fretting notes, try to get your finger as close to the fret as possible without being on top of it. This will produce clear, ringing notes with a minimum of buzzing or other unwanted noises.

The long, horizontal lines represent the strings. The top line is the 1st string (high E) and the bottom line is the 6th string (low E). Try fingering the notes indicated using any left-hand finger:

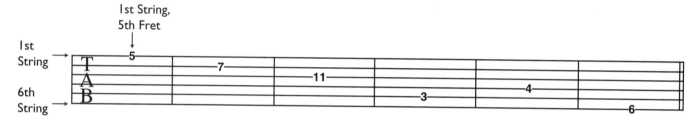

> **SECRETS OF THE MASTERS**
> *The dots on your guitar neck (if you have any) will help you keep track of the frets. The dots usually come on frets 3, 5, 7, 9 and 12. Look at your guitar and familiarize yourself with where the dots are.*

TAB is often attached to written music, so the player will know how long the notes last and what they are. The following examples show TAB and standard music notation. If you do not yet read music, DO NOT PANIC. If you like, you can look ahead to Chapter 2 (page 16) for information about reading standard notation. Or, just play the frets and strings indicated in the TAB in a slow, steady rhythm, giving each note equal length. The numbers under the TAB indicate the left-hand fingers (see page 7).

COWS THAT BOOGIE ON MY LAWN

Track 2

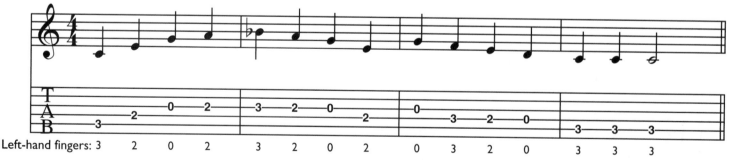

Left-hand fingers: 3   2   0   2   3   2   0   2   0   3   2   0   3   3   3

If you're looking for a fun challenge, put down that crossword puzzle and instead try to name the notes you are playing from the TAB. Use the musical alphabet from Lesson 2. In *This One's Got Spots*, the note names are given. In *Mary Had a Border Collie*, you're on your own.

THIS ONE'S GOT SPOTS

Track 3

MARY HAD A BORDER COLLIE

Track 4

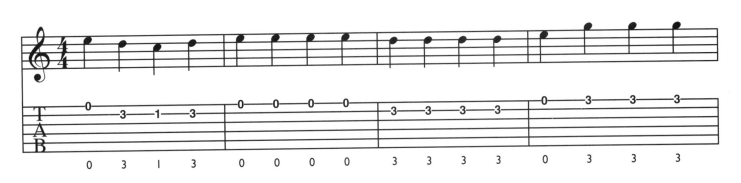

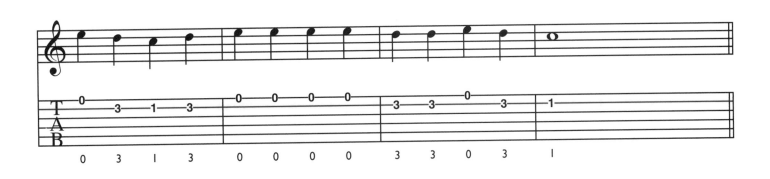

This lesson will get you started playing *chords* that you will use for the rest of your guitar-pickin' life. A chord is three or more notes sounded simultaneously. Each chord is named for the musical alphabet letter that serves as its *root*. The chords in this lesson are known as *open chords* because they use a mixture of *open* (unfingered) strings and fretted notes. They also occur in the first three or four frets of the fretboard.

> **SECRETS OF THE MASTERS:**
> *During this phase of your learning, it is more important to practice often than to practice for long periods. (For more on practicing, see page 94.)*

You will be building new pathways from your brain to your finger muscles. Like mountain trails, these paths need frequent clearing or they grow over and disappear. If you practice for 15-30 minutes every day, you *will* see improvement. On the other hand, if you wait several days between sessions, you will be starting at "ground zero" every time. It make take up to a few weeks before these chords start to feel natural. As you work on them, you may want to begin Chapter 2 to add some variety to your practice.

STRUMMING

One of the most common ways to play a chord is to *strum*. To strum, a pick, a single finger or all the fingers are moved rapidly across the strings, sounding them nearly simultaneously. A downstrum, indicated ⊓, is toward the floor. An upstrum, indicated ⋁, is toward the ceiling.

GUITAR CHORD DIAGRAMS

Guitar chords are most often depicted in *chord diagrams*. A chord diagram is like a picture of the fretboard that shows which strings, fingers and frets you will use to make your chord.

Note that a circle (○) over a string means to strum that string open as part of your chord. An "✕" over a string means to omit that string from the strum. Watch carefully for these symbols and make sure to follow them.

Here is a sample chord diagram and a photograph for comparison:

"D" Chord

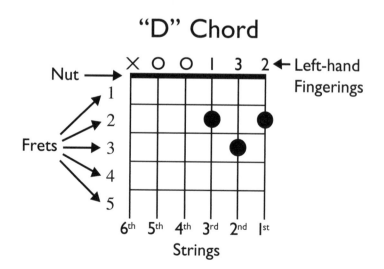

Here are your first three chords:

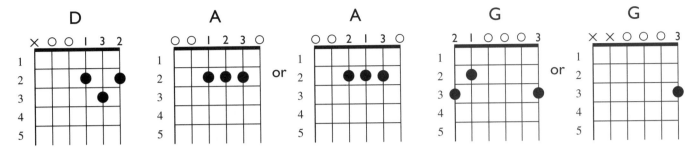

You may find that your fingers are too big to finger the A chord as shown. Try switching your 1st and 2nd fingerings so that the 1st finger is on the 3rd string, and the 2nd finger is on the 4th string. Some folks find that the G chord feels like too big a stretch at first. If that describes you, leave off the 2nd and 1st fingers, use the 3rd finger on the 1st string only, and strum just the upper four strings. When you are feeling a bit more limber, you can try the full chord form again.

Before you rush into trying to play your first song with chords, make sure that each chord is as clean and clear as it can be. While holding a chord with your left hand, pluck each string individually from the lowest string to the highest string. You may have to scoot your fingers around slightly to keep them from bumping into the adjacent strings or getting too far from or too close to the frets. Keep your fingers curved and your thumb behind the neck.

Once the chords are familiar, try strumming through *Canadian Campfire Song*. Use down strokes in time to a slow, even beat. It will help if you tap your foot and count the *beats* aloud. A beat is the basic unit of musical time. When you tap your foot, you are tapping the beats.

Canadian Campfire Song is written in *slash notation*. Each slash ╱ indicates one beat. The song is divided into groups of four beats called *measures*. *Bar lines* separate the measures. Change chords as indicated. For example, in the first measure, start with a D chord and change to an A chord on the third beat. Count slowly enough to allow for changing chords without stopping the beat.

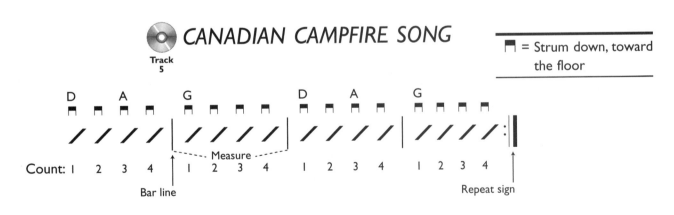

CANADIAN CAMPFIRE SONG

Track 5

▤ = Strum down, toward the floor

The repeat sign tells you to repeat the song from the beginning. Since this is a short sequence of chords, you may want to repeat it many times.

Remember, there is no need for physical pain and distress when learning the guitar. If your knuckles are turning white and there are shooting pains through your hands, you may be pressing too hard. Take it easy and your strength and accuracy (and calluses) will build in a short time.

LESSON 5: CHANGING CHORDS

Now that you've tried a few chords, here are some techniques to help your fingers learn to get to them faster:

FOUR-STEP FRETTING EXERCISE

This exercise is based on a classical guitar warm-up. Follow the steps slowly and steadily. Once you are familiar with the four steps, try them to the beat of a *metronome* set between 40 and 60 beats per minute. A metronome is an adjustable device used for determining the exact *tempo* (speed) of a piece. It is a great practice tool. (For more on metronomes, see page 93.)

1. Set .... Place your fingers lightly on the strings in the shape of the chord.

2. Press .... Press the fingers down on the frets simultaneously and strum the chord.

3. Set .... Relax pressure, without lifting fingers off strings.

4. Release .... Lift fingers off strings about $\frac{1}{8}$ inch, holding fingers in the shape of the chord.

Repeat this process several times.

This exercise is a great way to help your fingers learn the different chords faster. Try it every time you practice and with every new chord you learn. Another benefit is that you will learn to use only the minimum amount of pressure you need to play the chord; it doesn't take as much as you may think!

SWITCHING CHORDS

The secret to good chord switching is learning to move your fingers simultaneously from one chord to another. The exercise you just learned will help your fingers get used to acting together to press down a chord.

Moving your fingers precisely in different directions at the same time is no easy trick. In order to get the hang of it, it is helpful to look at the switching process with a magnifying glass. Each chord switch is like a tiny dance step for your fingers. Learn the first few steps very carefully and with some concentration, and the whole dance will get easier and easier.

For example, look at the switch from D to A.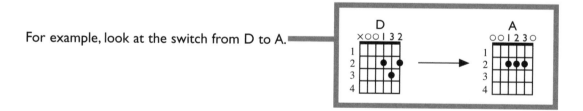

Make a D chord with your-left hand. Now look at your hand and imagine where the fingers will need to go to make the A chord:

- The 1st finger moves from the 3rd to the 4th string, staying on the same fret (the 2nd fret).
- The 2nd finger jumps from the 1st to the 3rd string, also remaining on the 2nd fret.
- The 3rd finger slides from the 3rd to the 2nd fret on the 2nd string. It doesn't even have to lift up from the string!

Now try to move from D to A using the four-step exercise.

| 1. Set the D chord.
| 2. Press the D chord.
| 3. Set the D chord.
| 4. Lift fingers together and move them in position for the A chord.

→

| 1. Set the A chord.
| 2. Press the A chord.
| 3. Set the A chord.
| 4. Lift fingers together and move them in position for returning to the D chord.

Though this process may seem a little intense, it is actually a short-cut to switching chords cleanly and quickly. A little patience, persistence and focus in the beginning will pay off! Use this technique with each new chord combination you encounter. Try it a few times with D, A and G, then go back to *Canadian Campfire Song* and behold the magic.

LESSON 6: MORE CHORDS—E AND C

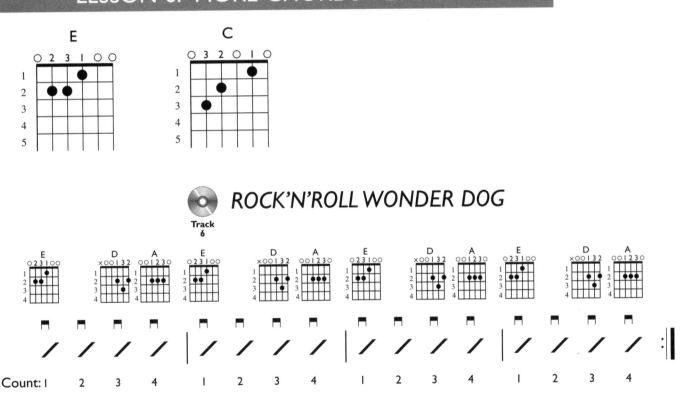

ROCK'N'ROLL WONDER DOG

Track 6

YOU MOVE MY BOOGIE MACHINE

Track 7

CHAPTER 2

Reading Music

HOW TO USE THIS CHAPTER

This chapter will provide a quick introduction to reading music in the first position of the guitar neck (the first four frets and open strings). You may want to work through this chapter at the same time you are learning to play and strum the chords in Chapter 3 (page 30). This will add variety to your practice. Most of the examples in this chapter do not have tablature. Tablature is used throughout the rest of the book. You do not have to master reading music in order to work on the other chapters, since TAB is always available.

WHY READ MUSIC?

Reading music is a rewarding skill that is easier to develop than most people think. It enhances tablature and chord charts by allowing you to read exact rhythms, vocal melodies and music for other instruments. Even the most basic understanding of the notes on the staff (Lesson 1, below) will give you a point of departure for the concepts introduced later in this book.

LESSON 1: THE NOTES AND THE STAFF

We use five horizontal lines as a sort of "playing field" for our notes. This is called the *staff*. The *natural notes* (notes without sharps or flats) are laid out on the lines and spaces of the staff. Lower notes are near the bottom of the staff, higher notes are near the top. A *clef* sign at the beginning of the staff indicates which notes are represented by which lines and spaces. When the *G clef* sits on the second line from the bottom of the staff it is called *treble clef*. The line it encircles is called G.

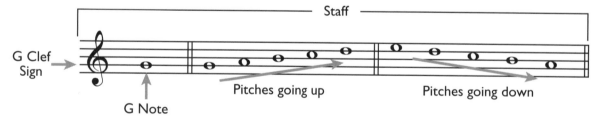

Now that you know the second line from the bottom is G, all the other notes can be related to that line. For example, the space under it is F, the note before G in the musical alphabet. The space above the G line is A, the next note in the musical alphabet.

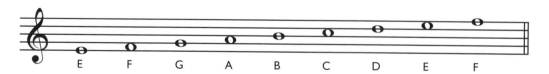

LEARNING THE NOTES ON THE STAFF

There are several memory devices you can use to quickly learn all the notes on the staff. One is to separate the notes on the lines and the notes in the spaces. The notes on the lines give you the first letter of each word of this sentence: "Every Good Beginner Does Fine." The notes in the spaces themselves spell the word "FACE."

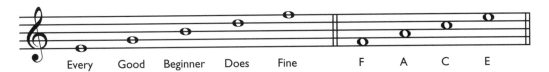

| Every | Good | Beginner | Does | Fine | F | A | C | E |

LESSON 2: THE NOTES ON THE 1ST STRING

Reading notes on the staff is easier when you learn a few at a time. Each of the following lessons will add a few new notes. The first three are on the 1st string. Here's where they are on the staff and on the guitar:

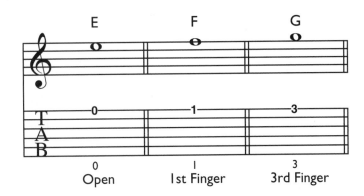

Here are some practice examples using E, F and G. First, make sure you can name all the notes easily. Then, try to play them in a slow, steady rhythm. Using your pick, play each note with a downward stroke. Use just the very tip of the pick, and don't hit the string too hard.

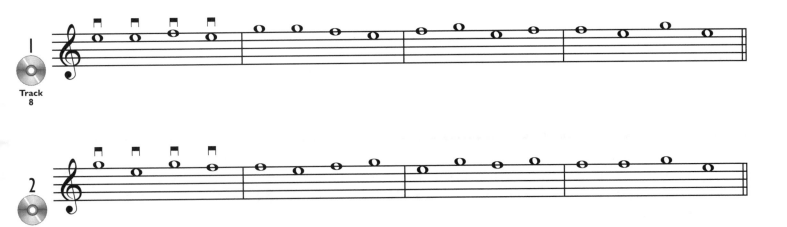

The first three notes on the second string are B, C and D.

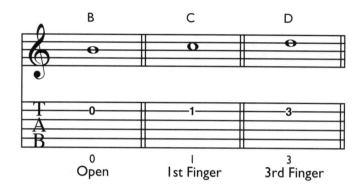

Try these playing examples. As in Lesson 2, pick all the notes with downstrokes. To speed along your learning, say the notes aloud before you play each line. Don't forget E, F and G! They return in these examples.

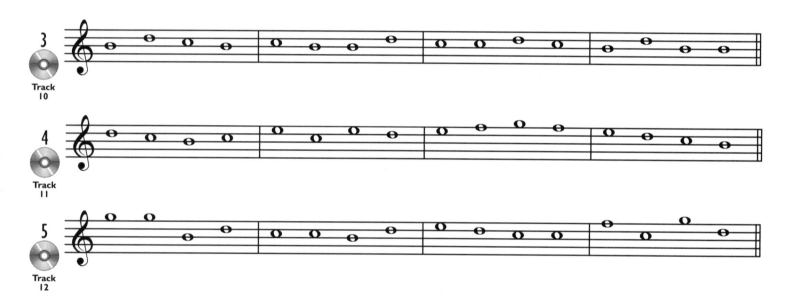

3 Track 10

4 Track 11

5 Track 12

LESSON 4: TIME

The first part of this is a quick review of material you learned in Chapter 1. Read it anyway, as there are important new details.

GET THE BEAT

The *beat* is the steady, even pulse that remains constant throughout a passage of music. It is what the listener's foot taps along to.

THE MEASURE

Musicians count beats and divide them into small groups. As you know, a group of beats is called a measure. Measures can consist of any number of beats. One very common measure is a group of four. Measures are marked on the staff using bar lines. For this reason, measures are sometimes called *bars*. A double bar indicates the end of a passage of music or short example.

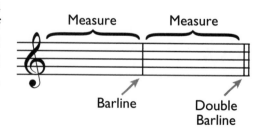

SIGNS OF THE TIMES

The *time signature* tells you how many beats are in a measure and which type of note gets one beat. It is found at the beginning of the piece. The upper number indicates the number of beats per measure. The lower number shows what type of note is one beat.

Time Signature

The time signature reads like a fraction, so $\frac{4}{4}$ could be read as "four quarters." This would mean that every measure has the equivalent of four quarter notes ♩, with each quarter note equaling one beat. Read on to learn about the different types of notes.

THE LONG AND SHORT OF IT

The *value* of a note is its duration (in beats). The appearance of a note tells us its value. Here are three note values and their durations:

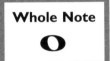

The *whole note* lasts for four beats. Try playing these and counting aloud. Remember to pick the note at the same time you say "one" and let it ring all the way through "two, three, four." Keep the beat steady and even. Tap your foot while you count!

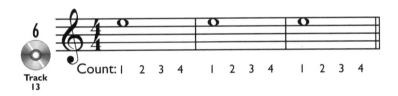

Track 13

Count: 1 2 3 4   1 2 3 4   1 2 3 4

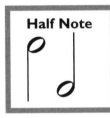

The *half note* lasts for two beats. In a measure of four beats, the half notes start on beats "1" and "3." Notice that notes with stems sometimes have the stems going up and sometimes have the stems going down. Normally, notes on or above the middle line have their stems going down, and notes below the middle line have their stems going up.

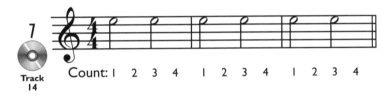

Track 14

Count: 1 2 3 4   1 2 3 4   1 2 3 4

The *quarter note* lasts for one beat. Play along with your counting.

Track 15

Count: 1 2 3 4   1 2 3 4   1 2 3 4

Now add D, E, F, G and A to your inventory of notes.

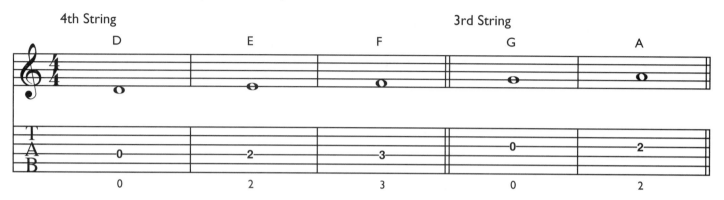

As you play these examples, remember the following:

1. Tap your foot in a slow, steady beat.
2. Count aloud.
3. Do not rush through the tunes. Give each note its full length.
4. Play each note with a downstroke of the pick.
5. Have fun. It's music!

Track 16

Track 17

Silence is as important a part of music as sound. The symbols that represent silence are called *rests,* and just like notes, they are measured into wholes, halves and quarters.

A *whole rest* is four beats of silence. It is a small rectangle that hangs like a full suitcase from the fourth line of the staff.

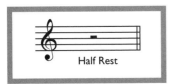

A *half rest* is two beats of silence. It is a small rectangle that sits like a hat on the third line of the staff.

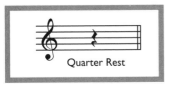

A *quarter rest* is one beat of silence. It looks a bit like a bird flying sideways.

> **SECRETS OF THE MASTERS**
> *Rests must be "played" with the same precision and importance as pitches! To play a rest, you must stop the string or strings from ringing by using your pick or lifting up a fretted note with your left-hand finger to stop the sound.*

The following examples use some of the notes and rests you've learned. Enjoy playing them.

LESSON 7: EIGHTH NOTES

The beat can be divided into smaller pieces to allow for faster notes. A quarter note can be divided into two *eighth notes*. Each eighth note lasts half of a beat. Eighth notes can appear alone (with *flags*) or connected in groups (with *beams*). The stems follow the same rules as for other notes: notes on or above the middle line of the staff have their stems going down, and notes below the middle line have their stems going up. An eighth rest looks like a slash with a small flag waving from it and it lasts for half a beat.

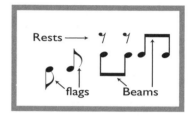

We can organize our note and rest values into a "tree" to help visualize the relationships.

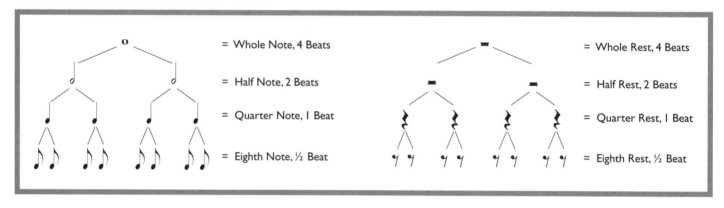

= Whole Note, 4 Beats

= Half Note, 2 Beats

= Quarter Note, 1 Beat

= Eighth Note, ½ Beat

= Whole Rest, 4 Beats

= Half Rest, 2 Beats

= Quarter Rest, 1 Beat

= Eighth Rest, ½ Beat

COUNTING EIGHTH NOTES

Eighth notes are counted by dividing the beats (counted "1, 2, 3, 4") into "1-&, 2-&, 3-&, 4-&." Tap on the numbered beats as before. Let's call these "on-beats" 👞 (sometimes called *downbeats*). Move your foot up on the "&s" ("ands"). These are called "off-beats" 👞 (sometimes called *upbeats*). Try clapping or playing this example on one note while you count and tap.

Count: 1 & 2 & 3 & 4 & 1 & 2 & 3 & 4 & 1 & 2 & 3 & 4 &

Tap:

WHAT GOES DOWN MUST COME UP

To play eighth notes, use a downstroke of the pick (⊓) for the down-beat, and an upstroke (∨) for the up-beat. As you play example 14, try to make the upstrokes sound identical in tone and quality to your downstrokes. Notice that your pick moves exactly the same as your tapping foot: down-up, down-up, down-up.

Track 20

Pick: ⊓ ∨ ⊓ ∨ ⊓ ∨ ⊓ ∨ ⊓ ∨ ⊓ ∨ ⊓ ∨ ⊓ ∨ ⊓ ∨ ⊓ ∨ ⊓ ∨ ⊓ ∨

Count: 1 & 2 & 3 & 4 & 1 & 2 & 3 & 4 & 1 & 2 & 3 & 4 &

> ### SECRETS OF THE MASTERS
> *Play as steadily as a Swiss watch! By using a consistant down-up motion, you will have an easier time keeping the beat and playing smooth, graceful lines at any speed. Make a lifetime commitment to even down-up picking!*

GOING DOWN LOW

In order to add the notes on the 5th and 6th strings, extra lines must be added to the staff. These are called *ledger lines*. As with the normal staff, a note may appear directly on a ledger line or in the space just below it. Here are the notes on the 5th and 6th strings.

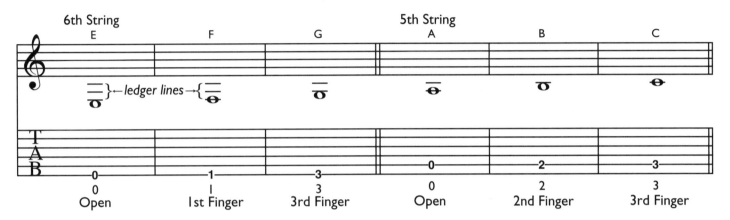

Examples 15, 16 and 17 will help you get used to reading notes with the ledger lines. Try to say the names of the notes aloud as you play them.

Notes on the 5th String

Notes on the 6th String

Notes on the 5th and 6th Strings

LESSON 9: EIGHTH RESTS AND DOTTED NOTES

THE EIGHTH REST

For every note value, there is also a rest. You have learned quarter, half and whole rests. Remember that an eighth rest looks like a slash with a small flag waving from it and it lasts for half a beat. Unlike eighth notes, eighth rests are not beamed together in groups. They always appear individually.

DOTTED NOTES

A dot placed after a note head increases its duration by half the value of the note. For example, a half note equals two beats. Half of that value is one beat so if we dot a half note, it equals three beats (2 + 1 = 3).

Dotted Half Note

The same logic applies to other note values. For example, a quarter note equals one beat. Half of that value is half a beat so a dotted quarter note equals one and one half beats (1 + ½ = 1½).

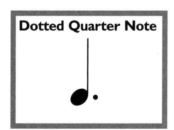

Dotted Quarter Note

Example 18 will give you some practice reading notes with dotted rhythms and eighth rests. To help you with the new rhythms, the counting is shown below the music. The numbers in parentheses are rests.

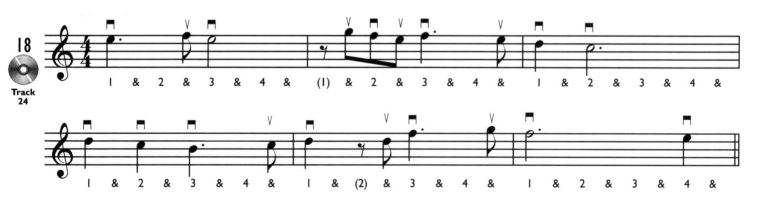

ACCIDENTALS DO HAPPEN

Once you have become familiar with reading the natural notes, adding the accidentals (sharps and flats, see page 8) is simple. Here's a quick review:

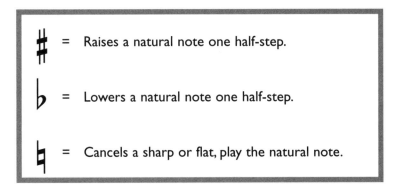

♯ = Raises a natural note one half-step.

♭ = Lowers a natural note one half-step.

♮ = Cancels a sharp or flat, play the natural note.

In written music, a sharp or a flat will appear just before the note it affects.

IMPORTANT NOTE:

When a sharp or a flat appears on a note, that note remains affected by the sharp or flat until the end of the measure. In other words, a sharp or flat can be canceled only by a natural or a bar line. Remember: a sharp raises a note by one fret; a flat lowers a note by one fret.

Example 19 introduces some of the sharps and flats in the first position. Tablature has been included to help you find these new notes.

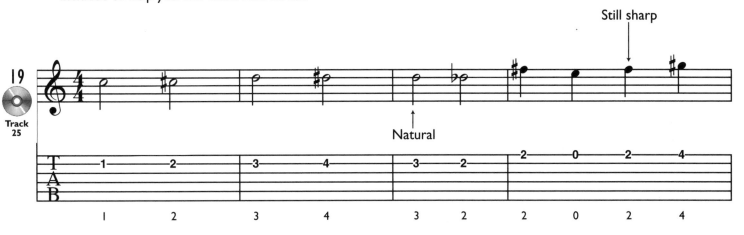

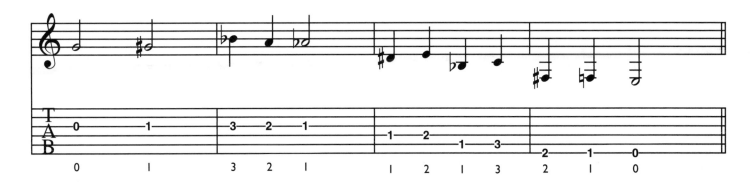

LESSON 11: READING KEY SIGNATURES

Most pieces of music have a *key*. A key is the *tonal center*—the note the piece revolves around. For example, in the key of C, the note C is the *tonic* or *keynote*. It's like home base for the key. When you learn about the *major scale* (page 46), you'll discover how a key is really composed of a whole set of notes from a scale and the relationships between them.

A *key signature* appears just after the clef sign at the beginning of each line of music. It is a set of sharps or flats (never both) that are always found in the scale of that particular key. The key signature is a form of shorthand that helps prevent the music from getting too cluttered with accidentals.

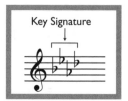

Key Signature

Reading a key signature is very simple. Look just to the right of the clef sign. Any sharps or flats that appear will affect that pitch throughout the entire piece of music.

For example, the key signature in the example on the right has an F♯ ("F sharp") and a C♯ ("C sharp"). This means that *all* of the F notes and *all* of the C notes will be sharped in this piece, unless otherwise marked.

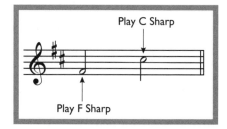

Play C Sharp

Play F Sharp

IMPORTANT NOTE:

Accidentals in key signatures affect the note in every octave, not just the line or space on which the accidental appears.

To learn which key signatures go with which keys, check out Chapter 5, staring on page 47.

Try these examples. Tablature has been included to help you find the new notes. In the first example, the pitches affected by the key signature have been circled. Circle the affected notes in the second example.

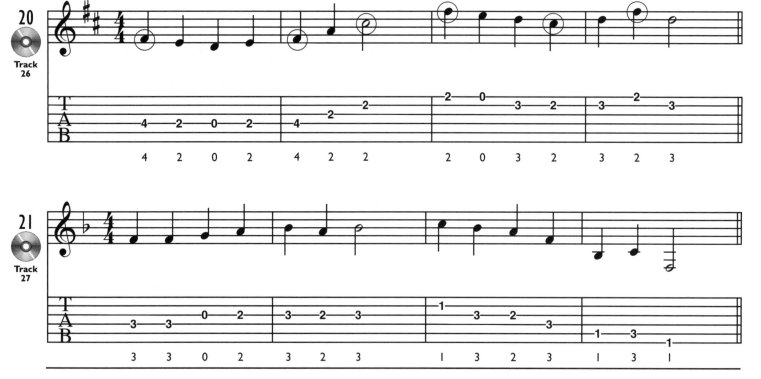

1st and 2nd endings are used to add variety to a repeated passage of music. The first time through, play the 1st ending, then repeat the passage. On the repeat, skip over the 1st ending and play the 2nd ending instead. The piece may end at this point or it may continue on to a new section. The piece below, *Line Dancing on Mars*, follows this form:

1. Play up to and including the 1st ending.
2. Go back to the beginning and play up to the 1st ending, *skip* it and play the 2nd ending instead.
3. Continue on in the piece and play the new section, starting at the right-facing repeat sign after the 2nd ending.
4. Repeat the new section.

Line Dancing on Mars uses many of the elements you have learned in this chapter, including accidentals, rests, dotted rhythms and notes on each string. In addition, it includes 1st and 2nd endings. There is no TAB here so that you can practice your note reading. Have fun!

 LINE DANCING ON MARS

Track 28

CHAPTER 3

More New Chords

LESSON 1: MINOR CHORDS

The chords you have already learned are called "major" chords. You will learn the theory behind what makes them "major" in Chapter 5 of this book. Major chords tend to have a bright sound and are sometimes associated with a happy or hopeful emotion. In this section, you will learn the "minor" versions of some of these chords. Minor chords have a darker quality that can have a sad, melancholy or even sinister emotion. Of course, these associations are highly subjective. As with diet plans and stock investments, results may vary from one listener to another.

Minor chords are often abbreviated with "min" or a small "m." In this book, for example, an A Minor chord is marked *Amin*. Here are your first three minor chords:

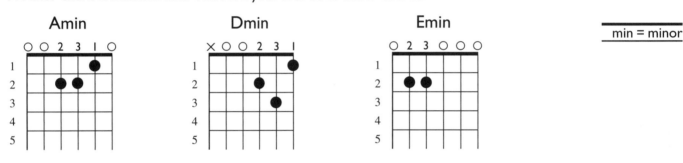

min = minor

Use downstrokes to strum the following progressions.

HEAVY FOG

Track 29

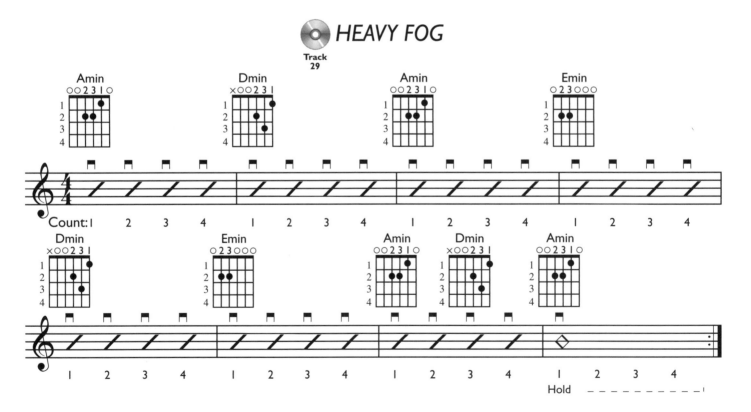

◇ = Whole note in rhythmic notation. Strum the chord once and hold it for four beats.

Minor chords can be mixed with major chords to give a more complete harmony and sense of movement to a song.

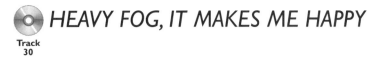

HEAVY FOG, IT MAKES ME HAPPY

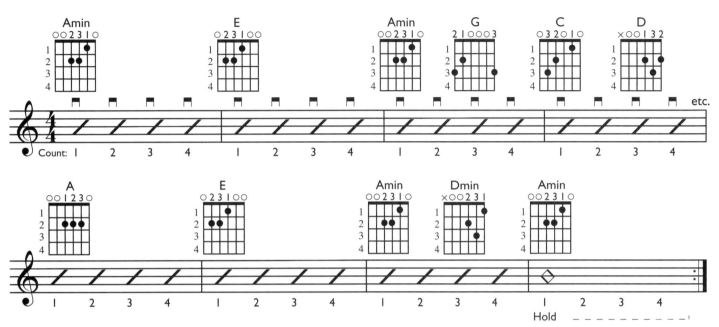

LESSON 2: THE BLUEGRASS G CHORD AND A C CHORD TO MATCH

BLUEGRASS G

Here's a new fingering for the G Major chord (page 13) you will definitely want to try. This fingering creates a new sound by putting the notes of the chord in a slightly different order. This version of the G chord has a big, bright sound. It is very common in bluegrass music. The early bluegrass guitar players often played in the key of G and used this voicing to cut through the sonic mayhem of banjos and fiddles. It has become a standard voicing used in rock, country and contemporary folk styles.

BLUEGRASS C

Try this new way of playing a C chord. It goes well with the bluegrass G chord because the G note on the 1st string is in both chords. This G note is called a *common tone* between the two chords.

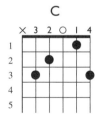

Try playing *The One-Human Garage Band*. To make it more fun, try strumming these chords with a firm snap of the wrist. This will make the chords louder and more percussive, and possibly frighten your pets. Remember that the two dots at the end mean repeat.

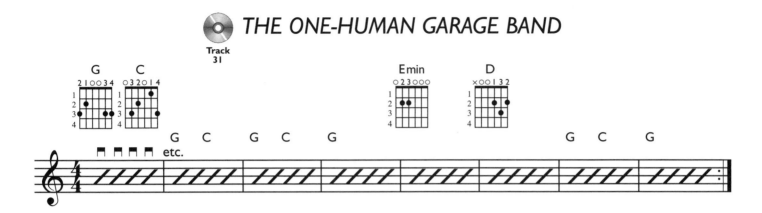

THE ONE-HUMAN GARAGE BAND

LESSON 3: THE ART OF STRUMMING

Once you are comfortable with at least a few of your basic chords, you can shift your attention from your left hand to your right hand and begin refining your strumming technique.

Here are some things to keep in mind when working on your strumming:

1. Keep your wrist loose and your arm relaxed.
2. Resist the urge to "tighten up" your muscles as you build up speed.
3. Work on developing a steady, even beat. You may want to try using a metronome (see the Appendix, page 93).

> **SECRETS OF THE MASTERS:**
> *To become a truly good rhythm guitarist you must develop an internal sense of rhythm that is steady and predictable. The best way to do this is to tap your foot on the beats and count aloud. Practice slowly and synchronize the movements of your hand with the tapping and counting.*

Rhythmic Notation
In the following examples, a new kind of notation is being introduced. This is a common way to show strumming rhythms when a specific rhythm is called for. The note values are indicated with slashes instead of circles for eighth notes and quarter notes, and with diamond-shaped heads for half notes and whole notes instead of open circles.

Whole   Half   Quarter   Eighths

Practice your strumming with the following rhythms:

Strum #1: Try this strum with a G chord using a steady down-up motion.

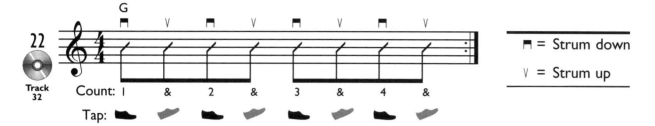

| | = Strum down
V = Strum up

Strum # 2: Here's one that mixes together quarter notes and eighth notes.

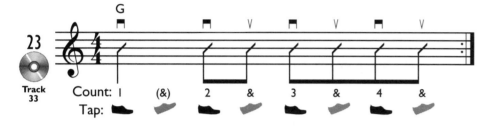

Strum # 3: Here's one that works well for folk songs and group singing. Also, try this with some of the progressions in earlier lessons.

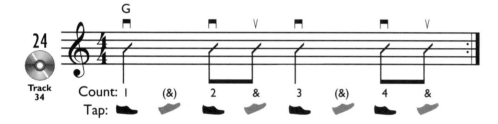

Train of Dreams is based on the folk song, *Midnight Special*. Play it with Strum # 3 (example 24). Remember to keep the beat steady! Use the bluegrass forms of G and C you learned on page 29. You may have to practice a bit to master switching between them.

TRAIN OF DREAMS

Track 35

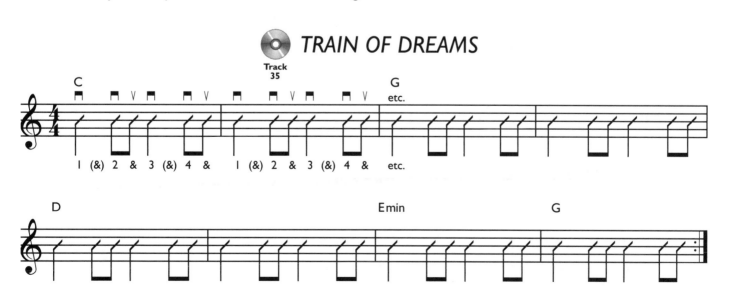

In the old days, the guitarist often had to serve the dual role of bass player and timekeeper. The roots of country, bluegrass and old-time guitar playing come from this style. The bass note of the chord is struck firmly, then the rest of the chord is strummed. What you get is the famous "boom-chick, boom-chick" rhythm.

Each chord has a *root* which the chord is named for. For example, the root of a C chord is "C." The root of an E chord is "E." You will want to play the lowest sounding root in the chord you are playing. Usually, we alternate between the root and another note called the "5th" of the chord. The "5th" is the fifth note above the root. For further explanation of the elements of chords, see Chapter 5 starting on page 45.

To help you, examples 25, 26 and 27 show the "boom-chick, boom-chick" strum written out on each chord you've learned so far. Repeat each one until it feels comfortable and secure. Note that on the C chord, you must move the 3rd finger to the 6th string to reach the alternating bass note.

Below are a couple of real live bluegrass tunes for you to try. Use the strum patterns you learned on page 32. Have fun!

BOIL THAT CABBAGE DOWN

Track 36

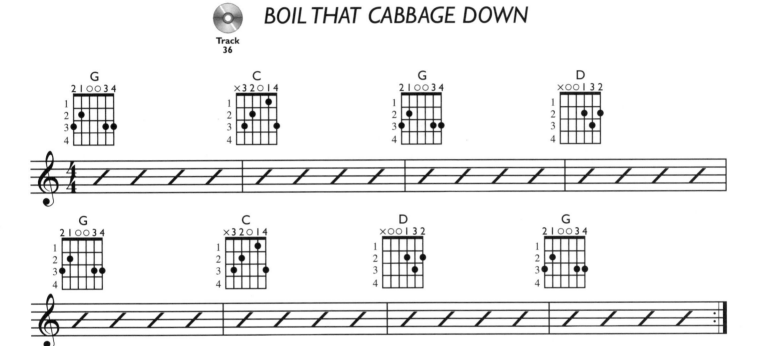

SHADY GROVE

Track 37

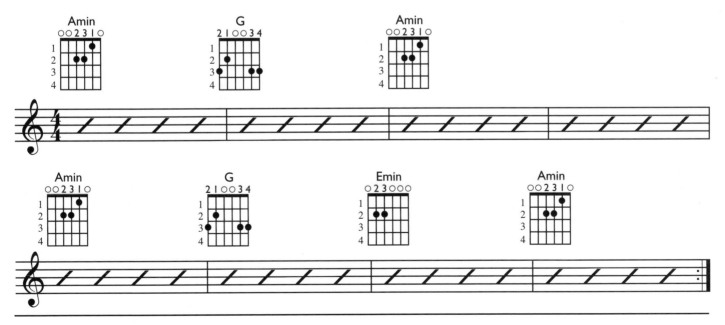

Flatpicking (playing with a pick) melodies is a staple of country, bluegrass and old-time playing. The early and middle twentieth century saw the guitar branching out from its role as a rhythm instrument. Jazz and blues players improvised solos on the guitar, while country and bluegrass pickers began to incorporate the fluid, agile melodies of fiddle tunes into their own playing. Now there are contests devoted solely to flatpicking acoustic guitar!

PRECISION WARM-UPS

The secret to good flatpicking is an absolutely steady down-up picking rhythm and clean, clear notes. Here are some warm-ups designed to help you develop the precision of your picking.

Warm-up #1: Groups of Four

This warm-up has four notes per string, picked down-up-down-up.

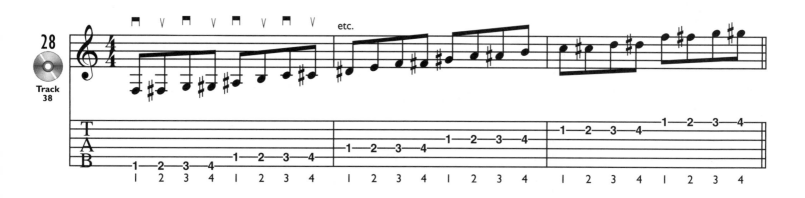

Continue this warm-up by repeating it in *second position* (the group of four frets beginning with the 1st finger on the 2nd fret), then third position and so on up the neck.

Warm-up #2: Groups of Three

This warm-up has only three notes per string. This will help you become fluent at beginning with both downstrokes and upstrokes when switching to a new string.

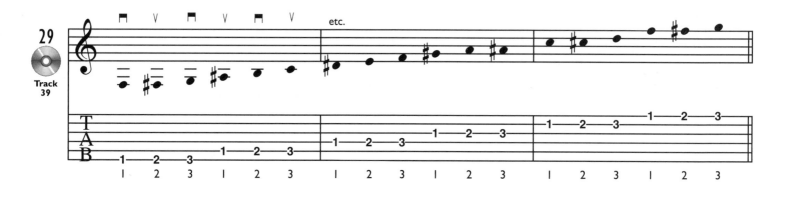

Sail Away Ladies is an old-time tune that can be heard at jam sessions across the country. The melody is shown in music and tab. The chords are indicated above the music. Use the country/bluegrass strum you learned on page 32.

This tune is written in the traditional, two-part fiddle tune form. There are two sections that we call *A* and *B*, respectively. Each section is repeated once and the whole tune is meant to be repeated many times. This is called a *binary form*. The form of the tune looks like this:
A   A   B   B

SAIL AWAY LADIES

Track 40

Syncopation means emphasizing the off-beats in a measure (also known as *upbeats*, page 22). In practice, this means that you will be emphasizing the "&s" of some beats, not just the numbered parts of the beats (the on-beats or downbeats). The end result is a rhythm pattern that rocks and rolls with groovy funkulence (if that's not a word, it should be).

TIES ONE ON FOR FUNK

In order to show syncopation in written music, dotted rhythms (see page 24) and *ties* are often used. A tie is a small curved line that connects two notes of the same pitch to create one longer note. Play the first note and hold it for its full duration plus the duration of the note to which it is tied.

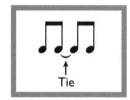

Notice that in the counting below the staff, the tied note is in parentheses.

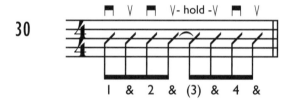

SYNCOPATED STRUM—IF YOU'RE ONLY GOING TO LEARN ONE STRUM...

...then this is it. Your newest strum is not just "Strum #4," it is The Universal Folk-Rock-Alternative-Swing-Funk-Campfire Strum. It is the Swiss Army knife of strum patterns. This is a good one at any speed, fast or slow. Note the tie that connects the "&" of beat 2 to beat 3. Be sure to tap your foot and count aloud. It's a good idea to tap your foot loud enough to hear an audible "thump" on beat 3, where the strings are not being struck. This will help keep you from speeding up every time you go from beat 2 to beat 3.

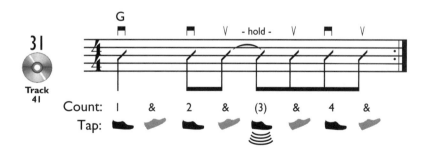

If you find this rhythm to be a little confusing, break it down into one or two beat segments:

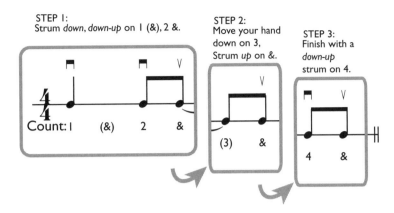

STEP 1:
Strum *down, down-up* on 1 (&), 2 &.

STEP 2:
Move your hand down on 3, Strum *up* on &.

STEP 3:
Finish with a *down-up* strum on 4.

The trick is to consciously move your hand down on beat 3 without hitting the strings. This keeps your hand movement regular and places your hand in the right place to strum up on the "&" of beat 3. Go slowly and keep a steady beat!

This strum has become a staple rhythm in acoustic (and electric) music. It can be heard on songs by R.E.M., The Wallflowers, Joni Mitchell, The Ramones, Steve Earle, Lucinda Williams, Lou Reed and countless others.

Below are a few chord progressions to try. Be patient when trying to switch chords while playing this strumming rhythm. Play slowly, keep your foot tapping and count aloud. Once it begins to feel natural, you can speed up. Try this strum on other chord progressions you come across in this book and in any other songbooks you may have.

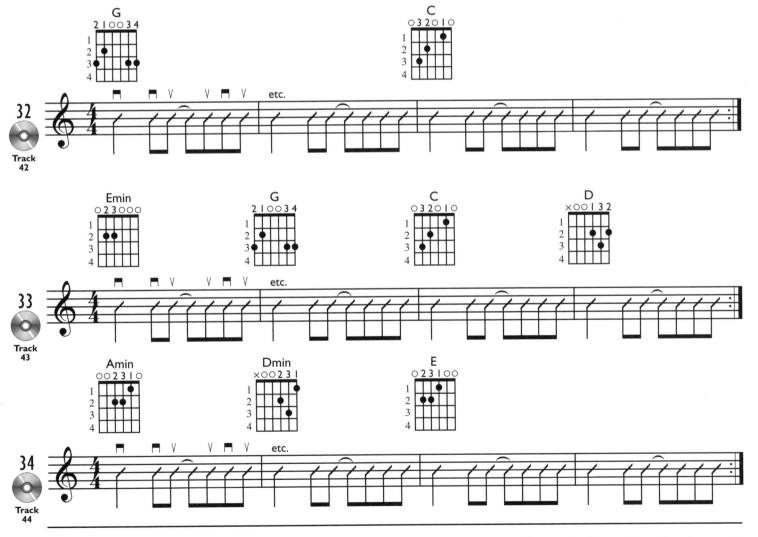

Waltz time is another name for $\frac{3}{4}$ time. This means there are three quarter notes in every measure. First, familiarize yourself with the feel of three beats per measure by counting and tapping your foot for a few bars:

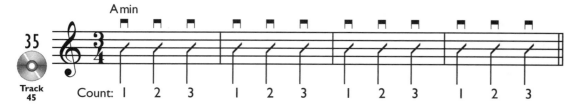

There are a variety of ways to strum in $\frac{3}{4}$ time.

Waltz Strum #1:

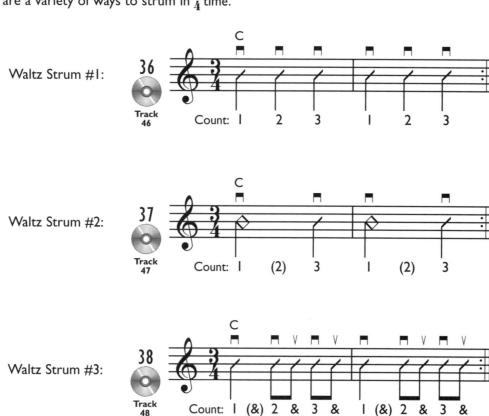

Waltz Strum #2:

Waltz Strum #3:

Waltz Strum #4: Country/Bluegrass (also known as "Oom-Pah-Pah"):

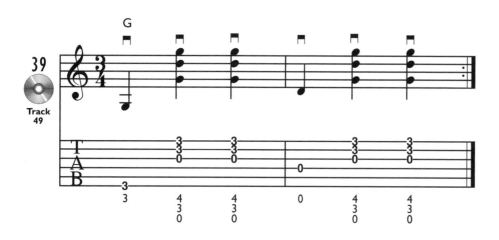

The gentle roll of waltz time can be particularly beautiful and lyrical. One of the most famous songs in $\frac{3}{4}$ is the traditional tune, *Amazing Grace*. Try the *Amazing Grace* melody. Then try the same chords with any of the waltz strums on page 38.

Note that the melody begins on beat 3. This is called a *pickup*. A pickup is a note or groups of notes that occur before the first full measure of a piece. Strictly speaking, where there is a pickup, there should be an *incomplete measure* at the end of the tune that balances out the incomplete pickup measure. In pop, rock, folk and other non-classical styles, this rule is not striclty adhered to.

Also notice the ties in the second and third lines. Play the first note, then hold it all the way to the end of the tied note. Do not strike the tied note. To review ties, see page 36.

AMAZING GRACE

Chapter 3—More New Chords   39

CHAPTER 4

Basic Fingerpicking

LESSON 1: THE RIGHT-HAND POSITION

Learning to fingerpick (playing *fingerstyle*) is a great way to overcome "the blahs" in your playing and try something new. Even a few basic patterns can provide textures that you can use for the rest of your life. Players such as Jewel, Steve Earle, John Prine and Tracy Chapman have used very basic fingerpicking to add a high level of impact to their songs. Others, such as Martin Simpson, Rory Block and Leo Kottke, have taken fingerstyle guitar to dazzling levels of complexity and expressiveness. If you find yourself drawn to the techniques touched on in this chapter, check out the *The Complete Fingerstyle Guitar Method*, also published by the National Guitar Workshop and Alfred.

RIGHT-HAND FINGERS

The most common method for naming the fingers of the right hand comes from the classical guitar tradition which uses the Spanish names for the fingers (***p***ulgar = thumb, ***i***ndice = index, ***m***edio = middle, ***a***nular = ring). All you have to memorize is the first letter of each.

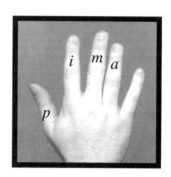

HOME POSITION

Contemporary acoustic and folk finger-
style playing is based on a basic "home position" that will allow you to play patterns and figures without turning your hand into a pretzel.

p ... plays the 4th, 5th and 6th strings
i .... plays the 3rd string
m .. plays the 2nd string
a ... plays the 1st string

THE RIGHT HAND WRIST

To achieve the best technical fluency possible (to maximize tone and minimize stress), it is helpful to understand some basic terms regarding the wrist:

ARCH	**ROTATION**	**TILT**
(up-and-down motion)	(side-to-side motion)	(Left-to-right motion from the elbow)

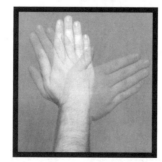

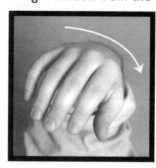

Your wrist should have a slight arch, little or no rotation and perhaps a slight tilt in towards your thumb. Keep your fingers relaxed and avoid tension in your forearm. If you feel tension or tightness, stop and "shake it out."

A good way to start fingerpicking is to learn a few repetitive patterns. These can be used with any chords you know. By placing your fingers in "home position," you can concentrate on which finger to play without worrying about which string to play.

If you find yourself getting tripped up, remove your hand from the guitar. Hold it up in the air and practice moving the fingers to the pattern while saying the right-hand pattern aloud a few times (for example: *p-i-m-a, p-i-m-a*, etc.). Then try it on the guitar again.

These patterns are called *arpeggios*. An arpeggio is the notes of a chord sounded one at a time. They can be played in an ascending, descending or more complex pattern. The patterns below are shown with C, G and D chords to help you practice moving the thumb to different root notes. Try them with all of your chords and with different songs and progressions!

ARPEGGIO PATTERN #1 — *p i m a*

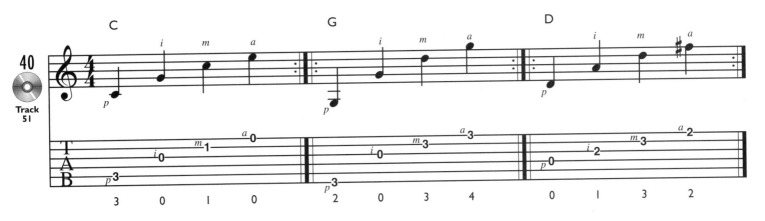

ARPEGGIO PATTERN #2 — *p a m i*

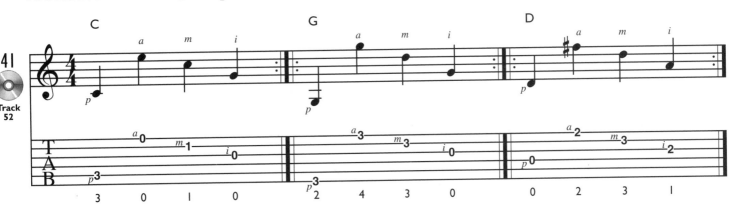

LESSON 3: ALTERNATING BASS PATTERNS

Alternating bass fingerpicking is a style that has roots in ragtime and blues piano playing from around the beginning of the 20th century. The thumb (*p*) plays the *bass* (the lowest note in the chord) and alternates between the root of the chord and the 4th string, while the fingers play with or between the thumb notes. On the D chord, *p* alternates between the 5th string (the 5th of the chord) and the root on the 4th string. Alternating bass is one of the most familiar and recognizable sounds in fingerstyle guitar, from blues and folk to pop, country and rock. It is also much easier to do than it sounds!

Below are a few very useful patterns to try. Practice them slowly at first. Played this way, they have an intimate sound that is good for ballads. Later on, as you gain confidence and speed up, they take on a rolling, syncopated quality. Also try making up your own patterns. Try different fingers in the spaces between the thumb notes.

ALTERNATING BASS PATTERN #1 — *p m p i*

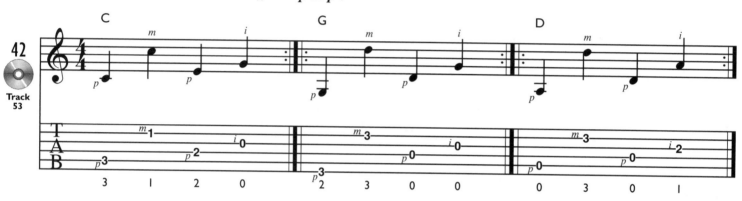

ALTERNATING BASS PATTERN #2 — *p a p i*

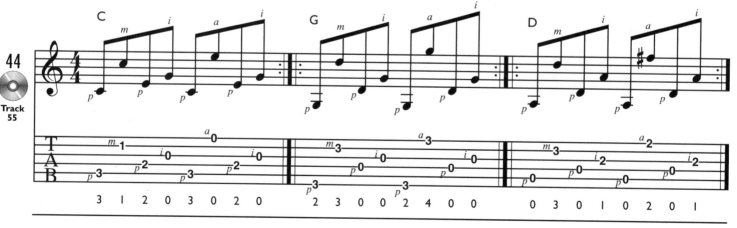

ALTERNATING BASS PATTERN #3 (COMBINATION OF #1 AND #2) — *p m p i p a p i*

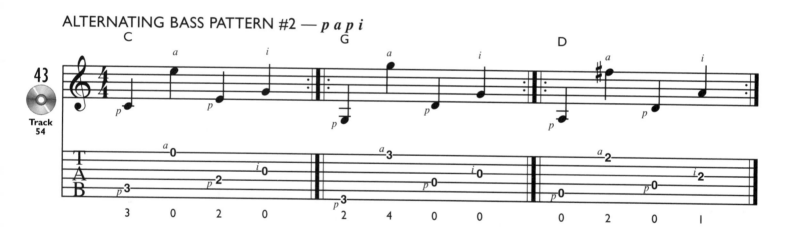

This tune will help you use your fingerpicking patterns in the context of a chord progression. Note that it uses a G/B chord in measures 2 and 9. This is a *slash chord*. This chord symbol is pronounced "G over B." It means that you are playing a G chord but the bass note is B (instead of the more common root G note). This chord allows your bass line to "walk" melodically from C (on the C chord) down to B (on the G chord), and then to A (on the Amin chord).

SLASH CHORDS

In a slash chord, such as G/B, the symbol to the left of the slash is the chord. The note to the right of the slash is the bass note (the lowest note played in the chord).

PRACTICE ROUTINE:

When you are working on putting a new technique to work in a song, try working on one measure at a time.

1. Practice the pattern of the first measure until you are very comfortable with it.
2. Practice measure 2 until you are very comfortable with it.
3. Now put together the two measures. Work on making a smooth transition between the two.
4. Start working on measure three, then add it to the other two. And so on...

CALIFORNIA FLOOD

Track 56

Some fingerstyle patterns work beautifully in $\frac{3}{4}$ time. Here are some patterns to try. Remember that you will only be counting to three! Try some of these patterns with the chords to Amazing Grace on page 39.

WALTZ FINGERPICKING PATTERN #1

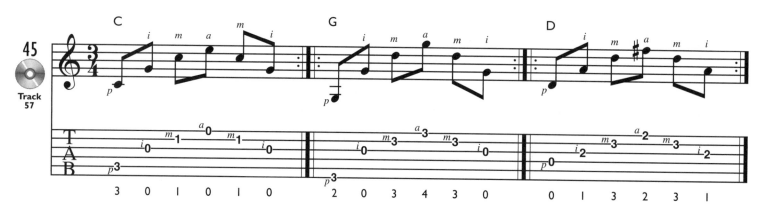

WALTZ FINGERPICKING PATTERN #2

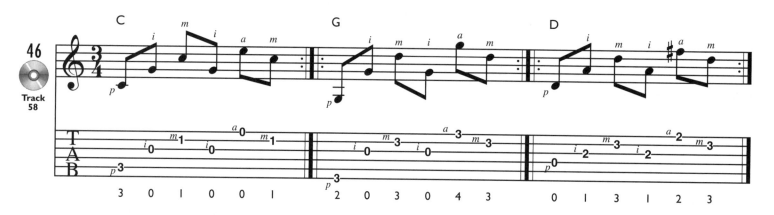

WALTZ FINGERPICKING PATTERN #3

Note that in this pattern, you will play your *a* and *m* fingers simultaneously. Some fingerpickers refer to this as a *pinch*. The technical term for two notes played simultaneously by a single instrument is *double stop*.

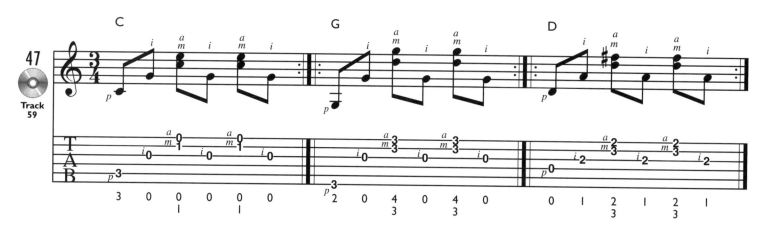

CHAPTER 5

Improvisation

Improvisation is the art of making up new music on the spot. It can be as simple as throwing in a new chord embellishment or strum pattern, or as complex as playing a free-form jazz solo. Improvisation is an important part of modern acoustic guitar playing. For example, many folk and blues players pride themselves on never playing a tune exactly the same way twice. Musicians in all styles use improvisation as a vehicle for expressing the emotions and attitudes of the moment.

> **Why Improvise?**
> • To add a sense of freshness and spontaneity to a performance.
> • To put your own personal expression into a piece of music.
> • To create a dialogue, or musical conversation, with another player.

TOOLS AND TECHNIQUES

There is no single, correct way to go about learning to improvise. You can base improvisation on your experience and knowledge of "what sounds good." On the other hand, you can throw caution to the wind and try to push the boundaries of your mind, ears and instrument. The best improvisers are able to do both.

> **There are some basic tools that can help you begin your journey:**
> • Theory
> • Imitation and analysis of players you admire
> • Playing with other people

A FEW WORDS ABOUT MUSIC THEORY

This chapter will give you some basic theory tools to start you on your way. Theory is the collection of terms and concepts we use to describe musical sounds and how they interact. Some people may fear that learning theory will ruin the spontaneity and creativity of their playing. Not so! Remember, knowledge can't hurt you!

> **What theory can do for you:**
> • Help you make connections between sounds you hear.
> • Broaden your possibilities for musical choices.
> • Help you explain your music to another player.

TAKING THE LEAP

When you combine a growing familiarity with theory, the study of players you admire and the experience of playing with others, you will build a foundation for limitless exploration of improvising. All that remains is to "take the leap into the unknown." When you are learning to improvise, try not to criticize yourself too much. Be fearless, open and have fun. Learn rules and break rules. This is not rocket science, it's music!

Willie Nelson became known as a leader of "outlaw country" in the 1970s. He combines bluegrass, blues and Texas swing with jazz inflections and phrasing.

PHOTO • CHUCK PULIN/COURTESY OF STAR FILE PHOTO INC.

LESSON 1: THE MAJOR SCALE

DOE, A DEER...

A *scale* is an arrangement of notes in a specific order of whole steps and half steps (see page 8). Of all the dozens of scales used in music, the *major scale* has the most instantly recognizable sound. It is the "standard of measurement" that musicians use in order to differentiate between all the other scales. In other words, we define all other scales by noting exactly how they are different from the major scale.

The sound of the major scale is that of the traditional "Do Re Mi Fa Sol La Ti Do" melody (made famous in the musical "The Sound of Music"). It has seven different notes, and uses each letter name from the musical alphabet (page 8) once—though some may be sharped or flatted. The first note, called the *tonic* (or sometimes *key note*) is repeated at the end, for a total of eight notes. The easiest major scale to learn is the C Major Scale, which uses no sharps or flats. Notice that the notes are numbered. These numbers are called *scale degrees*.

THE C MAJOR SCALE

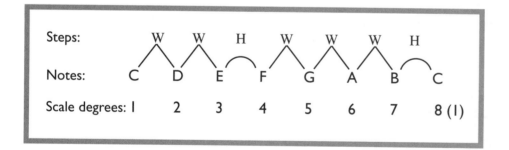

THE SECRET FORMULA

If you look at the C Major Scale as a series of whole steps and half steps, you will learn the "formula" for all major scales. Say it over and over to yourself and memorize it like you would your own phone number .

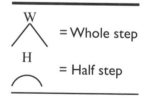

W		= Whole step
H		= Half step

IMPORTANT NOTE:

The notes of a major scale comprise the notes of a major key. For example, the notes of the C Major scale comprise the key of C Major.

"SPELLING" THE MAJOR SCALE IN ANY KEY—POP QUIZ

With careful use of the formula, you can *spell* (apply the formula of whole steps and half steps) the major scale starting on any note. Just start with the key note (1st scale degree) and then follow the formula, using each letter only once. The D Major scale is shown below. Notice that to make E to F a whole step, as the formula requires, we must raise the F a half step to F#. Try spelling the A and B♭ Major scales (the correct answers are at the bottom of the page).

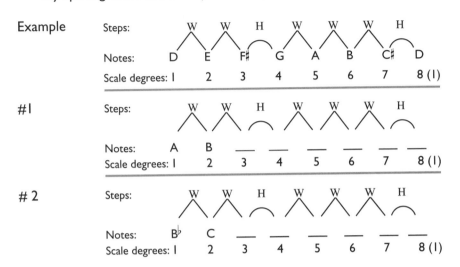

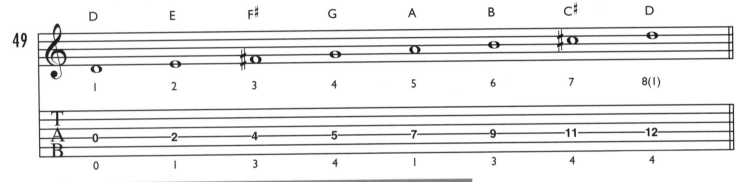

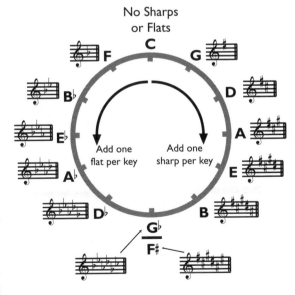

HOT TIPS:
1. Use every letter in the musical alphabet *once*, in alphabetical order.
2. The last note is the same as the first.
3. You will need to use either sharps or flats (never both) to make the notes fit the formula.

Try playing the D Major Scale by going up the 4th string. Playing the scale on a single string makes it easy to see the whole steps and half steps. The half steps are adjacent frets; for the whole steps, skip a fret. When you get comfortable with it, try it backwards!

LESSON 2: THE CIRCLE OF 5THS

The *circle of 5ths* is like the "secret agent decoder ring" of music theory. (And you don't have to send in any cereal box tops to get it!) A 5th is the distance between the 1st and 5th degrees of a scale. To make a circle of 5ths, just take the keys and arrange them in a circle so that the next keynote (going clockwise) is the 5th degree of the last scale. For example, the 5th degree of a B Major scale is F#, so the next key in the circle is F#.

The circle of 5ths makes it easy to learn the key signatures (page 26) for each key. The "sharp keys" (clockwise on the circle) add one sharp for each new key. The new sharp is always the 7th scale degree of that key. The "flat keys" (counterclockwise) add one new flat for each key. That flat is always the 4th scale degree of the key.

Notice that the keys of G♭ and F# are in the same position in the circle. The two scales are played on exactly the same strings and frets and sound exactly the same. Remember when two notes have the same sound but different names, they are *enharmonic equivalents*.

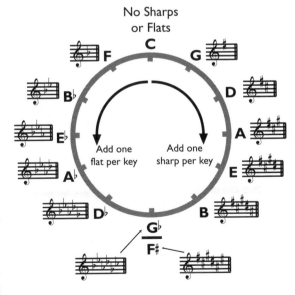

No Sharps or Flats

Add one flat per key

Add one sharp per key

In addition to playing major scales by going up one string, or playing in first position with open strings, we can play them across six strings with no open strings. We can catagorize these types of fingerings according to the finger we begin with. In this lesson, we will look at fingerings beginning with the 1st, 2nd and 4th fingers. There are three common ways of viewing each fingering: with finger numbers, note names or scale degree numbers. Let's look at the A Major scale starting on the 5th fret of the 6th string, with three different fingerings and three different views of each.

THE A MAJOR SCALE, STARTING WITH THE 1ST FINGER

FINGERING

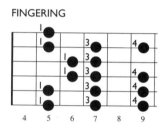

NOTE NAMES

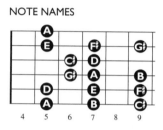

SCALE DEGREES

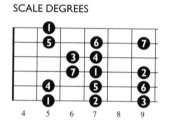

THE A MAJOR SCALE, STARTING WITH THE 2ND FINGER

FINGERING

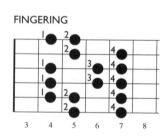

NOTE NAMES

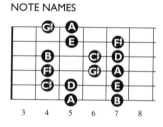

SCALE DEGREES

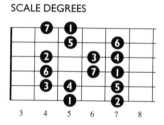

THE A MAJOR SCALE, STARTING WITH THE 4TH FINGER

FINGERING

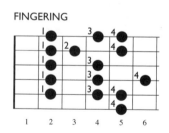

NOTE NAMES

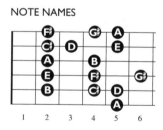

SCALE DEGREES

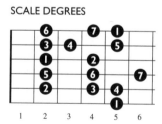

> **SECRETS OF THE MASTERS:**
> *Since there are no open strings in these fingerings, they are moveable. That means you can move them to any fret to play in any key. For example, the 6th fret of the 6th string is B♭. If you play these fingerings at the 6th fret, you need only change the names of the notes. Everything else—the finger numbers and scale degrees—remains the same.*

LESSON 4: THE MAJOR SCALE-DEGREE EXERCISES

Once you are very familiar with playing a scale fingering backward and forward, practice saying the scale degrees aloud while you play them. Then try some of these combinations of scale degrees. You might hear some familiar sounds or melodies!

Using your A Major Scale (any fingering), play the following scale-degree sequences:

A. 1-2-3   **F.** 7-6-4-5

B. 3-2-1-2-3-3-3   **G.** 1-3-5-3-1

C. 1-2-3-4-4-3-2-1   **H.** 2-4-6-4-2

D. 1-2-5   **I.** 5-7-4-6-3-1

E. 5-6-5-1

You can try these exercises in any key. Once your ear gets used to the sound of the new key, the melodies generated by the exercises will sound the same from one key to another (see **Secrets of the Masters** on page 48). Also try naming the pitches you are playing!

LESSON 5: IMPROVISING WITH THE MAJOR SCALE

The first step to improvising with the major scale is to become familiar enough with one of the fingerings that you can play it in your sleep. Then, begin to jump around within the scale, making up new melodies. Play some long notes and short notes, loud ones and soft ones. Don't worry about playing fast! Just try to get clean, clear notes that flow smoothly from one to another.

EAR TRAINING

Ear training is an integral part of learning music. A well-trained ear is what allows an improviser to transfer sounds from the imagination to the instrument. You can do some of this on your own, in the privacy of your own home. Look for opportunities to do this kind of work.

SING, SING, SING

The simple truth: The key to ear training is singing. Using a simple syllable such as "La" or "aaaah," try to *match* (sing) the pitches you are playing on your instrument. When practicing scale exercises, sing the numbers of the scale degrees as you play them. Try to sing a simple melody such as *Mary Had a Little Lamb* and play it by ear on your guitar.

Do a little "ear practice" every day. Also, enlist the help of a teacher if you can.

SECRETS OF THE MASTERS: A scale is only a bunch of whole steps and half steps! The magic of a scale is unlocked when you begin to explore the infinite melodies that lie within it. Simply learning to fly up and down scale fingerings may be fun for your fingers but it won't be very musically satisfying. Try to use your voice, your ear and your guitar to discover how melodies are put together, where they flow and where they skip around, where they start and where they end.

LESSON 6: INTERVALS

An *interval* is the distance between two pitches. You already know three intervals: the whole step (which in interval lingo is a *major 2nd*), the half step (*minor 2nd*) and the 5th (seven half steps). Intervals are best understood relative to a scale. For example, the distance from the 1st degree to the 2nd degree of a scale is an interval of a 2nd; from the 1st degree to the 3rd degree of a scale is an interval of a 3rd, and so on.

INTERVAL QUALITY

Every interval has a *quality*. The quality is the type of sound it makes, such as major or minor. Don't panic! The qualities will be disussed in greater detail in Lesson 7. The major scale generates only major and perfect intervals when measuring up from the tonic (1st degree):

INTERVALS IN THE MAJOR SCALE		
From the 1st Degree to the:	Interval	Abbreviation
1st Degree	Perfect Unison	PU
2nd Degree	Major 2nd	M2
3rd Degree	Major 3rd	M3
4th Degree	Perfect 4th	P4
5th Degree	Perfect 5th	P5
6th Degree	Major 6th	M6
7th Degree	Major 7th	M7
8th Degree	Perfect Octave	P8

Here are the intervals from the major scale in standard notation:

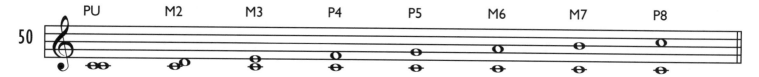

Each interval quality can be measured in half steps. For example, a major 2nd (whole step) equals two half steps. A major 3rd equals four half steps. There are also other kinds of intervals besides major or perfect. If you make a major interval smaller by one half step, it becomes minor. For example, C to E is a major 3rd (four half steps), but C to E♭ is a minor 3rd (three half steps). If you make a perfect interval smaller, it becomes diminished; if you make it bigger, it becomes augmented. Here is a chart showing all the intervals and their measurements in half steps, plus examples measured up from C and up from A.

INTERVALS FROM THE UNISON TO THE OCTAVE				
Interval	Abbreviation	Half Steps	From C	From A
Perfect Unison	PU	0	C	A
Minor 2nd	m2	1	D♭	G♭
Major 2nd	M2	2	D	B
Minor 3rd	m3	3	E♭	C
Major 3rd	M3	4	E	C♯
Perfect 4th	P4	5	F	D
Augment 4th or Tritone	Aug4 or TT	6	F♯	D♯
Diminished 5th or Tritone	dim5 or TT	6	G♭	E♭
Perfect 5th	P5	7	G	E
Minor 6th	m6	8	A♭	F
Major 6th	M6	9	A	F♯
Minor 7th	m7	10	B♭	G
Major 7th	M7	11	B	G♯
Perfect Octave	P8	12	C	A

Here are the intervals from the unison to the octave, measured up from C, in standard notation:

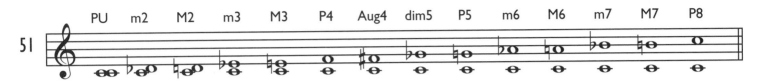

Here are the intervals from the unison to the octave, measured up from A, in standard notation:

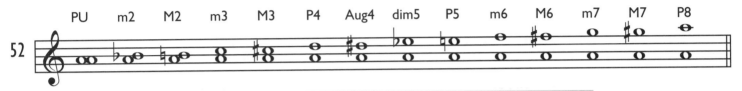

Don't Panic! Lesson 7 will allow you to play, hear and understand the intervals in easy doses.

INTERVAL INVERSION

Each interval can be *inverted*. To invert an interval, we simply take the bottom note and put it on top (or vice versa). For example, if we take C up to E (a major 3rd) and put the C on top so that it is now E up to C (a minor 6th), we have inverted the interval. The numbers of an inverted interval always add up to 9 (a 3rd inverts to a 6th; 3 + 6 = 9). Also, when inverted, major intervals become minor and minor intervals become major. Diminished intervals become augmented and vice versa. Perfect intervals remain perfect (that's what's perfect about 'em).

This table can be read right to left and left to right.

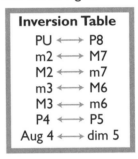

Inversion Table		
PU	⟷	P8
m2	⟷	M7
M2	⟷	m7
m3	⟷	M6
M3	⟷	m6
P4	⟷	P5
Aug 4	⟷	dim 5

Here are the interval inversions, all beginning with an interval built on C, in standard notation:

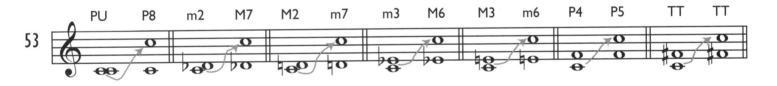

CONSONANCE AND DISSONANCE

Intervals are often described by the qualities of their sound. A *consonant* interval has a harmonious sound that produces a feeling of rest or *resolution*. There is no feeling that further musical movement is required. Consonant intervals include PU, P8, m3, M3, m6, M6 and P5. A *dissonant* interval has a clashing sound that produces an unresolved feeling called *musical tension*. Dissonance asks for musical movement to a point of *resolution*. Dissonant intervals include m2, M2, TT, m7 and M7. A P4 can be considered either a consonance or dissonance, depending on the context.

It is the fluctuation between "tension" and "resolution" that gives music a sense of motion, direction and emotional effect.

LESSON 7: FINGERINGS FOR INTERVALS

Learning intervals on the fingerboard can take a little work but it will help you to thoroughly master the instrument. It is easy if you concentrate on one or two interval types at a time.

To make things consistent in this lesson, each interval fingering is indicated for the same set of pitches (for example, all of the perfect octave fingerings are for A to A). You will be able to hear that each fingering generates the same pitches. Play the notes shown in the fingerings one after another (*melodically*) and simultaneously (*harmonically*), and get used to the sounds of the different intervals.

PERFECT OCTAVES

PERFECT OCTAVE = 12 HALF STEPS
Below are the fingerings for a perfect octave. The frets indicated will sound the notes A and A.

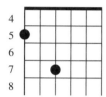 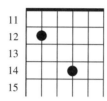 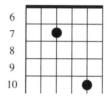 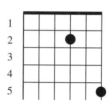

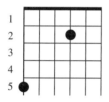 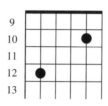 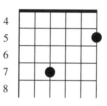

Octaves are one of the best interval shapes to memorize. They are important in blues and funk riffs and in the styles of contemporary players like Ani DiFranco and Dave Matthews. When the two notes are played simultaneously, the octave shape can be moved up or down the neck to create melodies. We call these *parallel octaves*. A master innovator in this style of playing was the jazz guitarist, Wes Montgomery. An octave corresponds to the first two notes of the *Somewhere Over the Rainbow* from "The Wizard of Oz."

Finally, octaves can help you learn the notes on the fingerboard much faster. Every time you learn a note, use the octave shapes to find other locations of the same pitch on the fingerboard.

PERFECT 4THS, PERFECT 5THS AND TRITONES

PERFECT 4TH = 5 HALF STEPS
Below are the fingerings for the interval of a perfect 4th. The frets indicated will sound the notes A and D.

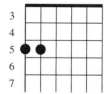 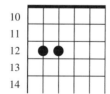 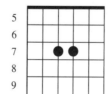 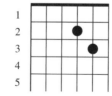 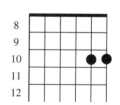

The perfect 4th is the distance between each of the open strings (except between the 3rd and 2nd strings). Perfect intervals have a resonant, "in tune" sound. The perfect 4th interval correspond to the first two notes of the melody to *Here Comes the Bride* (*The Wedding March* by Felix Mendelssohn, 1809-1847). It can be inverted to form a perfect 5th.

PERFECT 5TH = 7 HALF STEPS

Below are the fingerings for the interval of a perfect 5th. The frets indicated will sound the notes D and A.

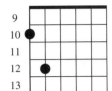 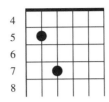 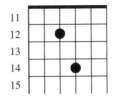 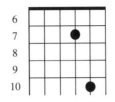 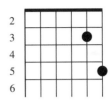

The perfect 5th is also known to guitarists as the *power chord* (page 80). When played on the lower strings, the shape can be moved around to play basic, "stripped down" chord progressions. Power chords are named after the lower note. For example, a perfect 5th with D as the low note is known as a *D Power Chord* or *D5*. The perfect 5th corresponds to the first two notes of a melody from *Also sprach Zarathustra* by Richard Strauss (1864-1949) which was used in the movie, "2001: A Space Odyssey." The perfect 5th can be inverted to form a perfect 4th.

TRITONE = 6 HALF STEPS

Here are the fingerings for the interval of a tritone. The frets indicated sound the notes A to D#.

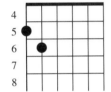 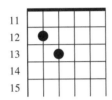 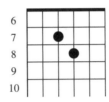 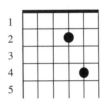 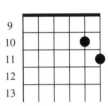

The tritone is a very special interval. It divides the octave equally in half. In other words, the distance from A to D# is the same as the distance from D# to A (six half steps—three whole steps, hence the name). This means that a tritone inverted is still a tritone.

The tritone is the most unstable-sounding interval, even though it is not necessarily the most dissonant. The tritone carries a lot of tension. Try playing a tritone and then moving each pitch by one half step in opposite directions. Hear the tension resolve!

The tritone is halfway between the perfect 4th and perfect 5th. Therefore, it is also known as an augmented 4th (one half step larger than a perfect 4th) or a diminished 5th (one half step smaller than a perfect 5th), depending on whether the note is sharp or flat.

The first two notes of the melody to *Maria* from the musical play "West Side Story" by Leonard Bernstein are a tritone. The two pitches of the tritone can be alternated to imitate the characteristic sound of European ambulance sirens in World War II movies.

2NDS AND 7THS

MINOR 2ND = 1 HALF STEP

Below are the fingerings for the interval of a minor 2nd or half step. The frets indicated sound the notes A and B♭.

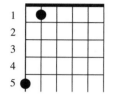 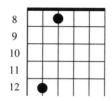 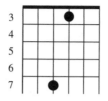 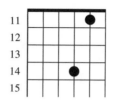 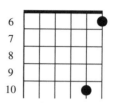

Minor and major 2nds are the building blocks of scales and melodies. Minor 2nds, when played harmonically, are among the most dissonant of intervals. Try moving a minor 2nd shape up and down the neck, playing a melody in parallel minor 2nds. Unless the sound of fingernails on a blackboard bothers you, this can be a cool effect. The minor 2nd corresponds to the first two notes of the theme to the movie "Jaws" by John Williams. The minor 2nd can be inverted to form the major 7th.

MAJOR 7TH = 11 HALF STEPS

Below are the fingerings for the interval of a major 7th. The frets indicated will sound the notes B♭ to A.

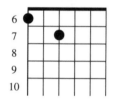 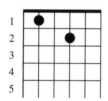 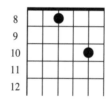 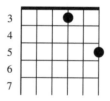

The major 7th is the inversion of the minor 2nd. A major 7th sounds the interval between the first and third note of first two notes of *Bali-Ha'i* from the musical "South Pacific" by Rodgers and Hammerstein. A major 7th can also be thought of as "one half step below an octave." To try this, make an octave shape and move the higher note down one half step. Whammo—major 7th!

MAJOR 2ND = 2 HALF STEPS

Here are the fingerings for the major 2nd (whole step). The frets indicated will sound the notes A to B.

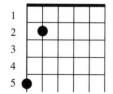 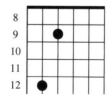 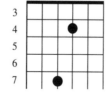 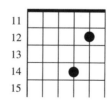 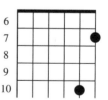

The major 2nd, as mentioned above, figures heavily in constructing scales and melodies. The major 2nd corresponds to the first two notes of *Amazing Grace* (page 39). The major 2nd can be inverted to form the minor 7th.

MINOR 7TH = 10 HALF STEPS

Here are the fingerings for the interval of a minor 7th. The frets indicated will sound the pitches B to A.

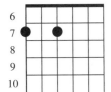 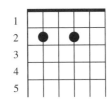 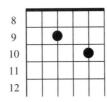 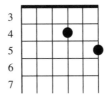

7ths are important intervals in coloring blues and jazz chords and melodies. The minor 7th can also be thought of as "one whole step below the octave." Try making an octave shape and move the higher note down one whole step. The minor 7th corresponds to the first two notes of the song *Somewhere* from Leonard Bernstein's "West Side Story." The minor 7th can be inverted to form the major 2nd.

*While still a teenager, **Ani DiFranco** appeared on the New York folk scene of the late 1980s. A prolific writer and recording artist, DiFranco is a leader in the world of independent music. Her rhythmic, forceful guitar style makes use of alternate tunings, funk rhythms and unusual chord voicings. She uses in-concert improvisations and jam sessions with her band to develop new material.*

3RDS AND 6THS

MINOR 3RD = 3 HALF STEPS

Here are the fingerings for the interval of a minor 3rd. The frets indicated will sound the notes A and C.

 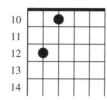 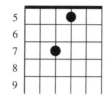 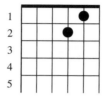 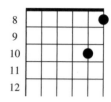

Minor and major 3rds are the building blocks of chords, including all of the chords you now play (see page 58). The minor 3rd corresponds the interval from the second to the third notes of the melody to the famous lullaby by Johannes Brahms (1833-1897), now called *Brahms' Lullaby* ("go to sleeeeeeep, go to sleeeeeeep...."). The minor 3rd can be inverted to form the major 6th.

MAJOR 6TH = 9 HALF STEPS

Below are the fingerings for the interval of a major 6th. The frets indicated will sound the notes C and A.

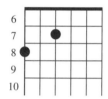 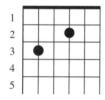 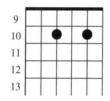 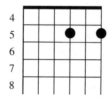

Both 3rds and 6ths are used to create harmonies for melodies. Major and minor 6ths are often used on the higher strings to give a "country harmony" sound that brings to mind the clean, twangy guitar sounds of Nashville. The major 6th corresponds to the first two notes of the melody to *My Bonnie Lies Over the Ocean*. The major 6th can be inverted to form the minor 3rd.

MAJOR 3RD = 4 HALF STEPS

Here are the fingerings for the interval of a major 3rd. The frets indicated will sound the notes A and C♯.

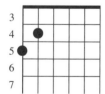 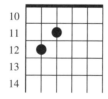 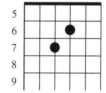 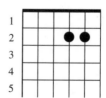 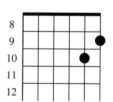

The major 3rd, with the minor 3rd (and their inversions, the 6ths) are crucial to building chords and harmonies. The major 3rd corresponds to the first two notes of the chorus of *Ob-la-di, Ob-la-da* by the Beatles, the guitar riff on *Blister in the Sun* by the Violent Femmes and the guitar riff to *Stir It Up* by Bob Marley. The major 3rd can be inverted to form the minor 6th.

*Known since the 1960s as the arm-swinging, guitar-smashing rock hero of the Who, **Peter Townshend** also developed an acoustic approach to communicate the intensity and emotion of a full-strength rock band. Townshend's style combines flamenco-style strumming, cross rhythms and bluesy leads. His acoustic work is a defining feature of the Who's album, "Tommy," (1969) and of many other recordings.*

MINOR 6TH = 8 HALF STEPS

Here are the fingerings for the interval of a minor 6th. The frets indicated sound the notes C# and A.

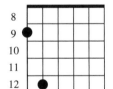 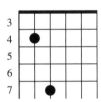 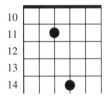 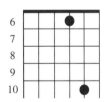 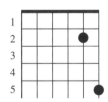

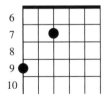 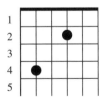 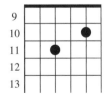 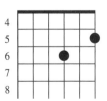

The minor 6th interval, when played melodically (one note at a time), has an unresolved quality that makes it easy to confuse with the tritone. But when the notes are played simultaneously, a very consonant sound emerges. The minor 6th can be inverted to form the major 3rd. The minor 6th corresponds to the first two notes of *Where Do I Begin* by Francis Lai from the movie "Love Story."

LESSON 8: HARMONY AND CHORDS

As you know, a chord is any three or more notes played together. The subject of chords and how they behave is called *harmony*. The most basic kind of chord is called a *triad*. A triad is a three-note chord, generally made by stacking one interval of a 3rd on top of another. All of the chords you have learned so far in this book are triads. Even though you may play all six strings, there are only three different notes; some are just repeated.

Below is a C Major scale that has been *harmonized*. This means that 3rds have been stacked above each note of the scale to form triads. The harmony notes are all within the scale—no sharps or flats have been added or changed. This is called *diatonic harmony*, or harmony within the key. TAB has been included so it will be easy for you to hear what the harmonized scale sounds like. You can also play the same chords any other way that is familiar and comfortable for you. You will find three types of triads—major, minor and diminished, which are all discussed below.

THE HARMONIZED C MAJOR SCALE

dim = Diminished

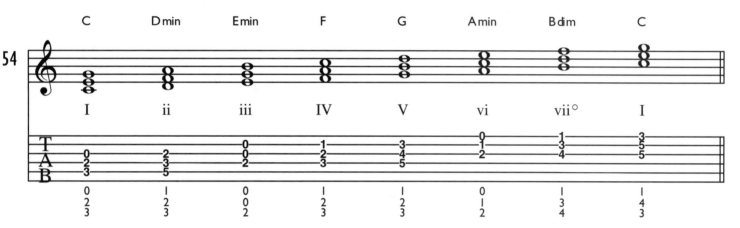

Notice that the chords have been numbered with Roman numerals. This allows for a distinction between scale degrees and chord numbers. The Roman numerals also show the quality of the chord. Check out the chart on the right.

Roman Numeral Review			
I .....i*.....1		V ...... v 5	
II .... ii 2		VI..... vi 6	
III ... iii ... 3		VII ... vii ...7	
IV ... iv 4			

* Lower-case Roman numerals are used for minor and diminished chords.

THREE KINDS OF TRIADS

The three types of triads that result from harmonizing the major scale are all made with different combinations of major and minor 3rds.

- A major triad is a major 3rd with a minor 3rd on top.
- A minor triad is a minor 3rd with a major 3rd on top.
- A diminished triad is a minor 3rd with another minor 3rd on top.

The bottom note of the triad is called the *root*. The middle note, which is a 3rd above the root, is called the *3rd*. The top note, which is a 3rd above the 3rd and a 5th above the root, is called the *5th*.

For easy comparison, example 55 shows all three triad types built on a C root.

5th
3rd
Root

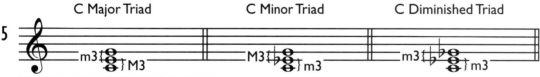

THREE PRIMARY CHORDS

The *primary chords* in every major key are the I, IV and V (one, four and five) chords.

Here is a D Major scale with the roots of the I, IV and V chords circled.

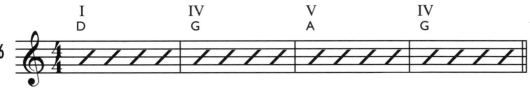

Here is a chord progression using I, IV and V. The key of D Major is indicated. Also try it in G and A. Use any chord fingerings or strum patterns you like.

Key of D Major

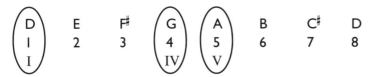

Key of G Major
Fill in the blanks. The answers are at the bottom of the page.

Key of A Major
Fill in the blanks. The answers are at the bottom of the page.

THE TRIUMPHANT RETURN OF THE CIRCLE OF 5THS

The circle of 5ths can be used to show basic harmonic movement. Instead of keys, these are major chords. Box or circle any three adjacent chords. The one in the middle is I. The one going clockwise is V. The one going counter-clockwise is IV.

Now that you have experimented a bit with intervals, the major scale and chords, it's time to make the magic happen!

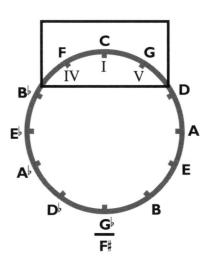

ANSWERS

Key of G: G C D
            I IV V

Key of A: A D E
            I IV V

This lesson is going to use a chord progression in the key of A. Roman numerals are provided so that you can try it in other keys. Use any strum rhythm you like. Here is the chord progression:

LAUNCHING THE PLANE SEQUENCE

Improvising a solo melody is a little (very little) like flying a plane. You have to get off the ground, fly around for a while and then come in for a landing. Scale passages are one of many good ways to get going.

One fun thing to do is break the scale into small pieces and then move the pieces up the scale. In other words, we can take a small idea, called a *motive*, then repeat it starting on other scale degrees (either higher or lower). This is called a *sequence*. Imagine yourself walking upstairs. Instead of running straight up, you go up three steps and back one, then up three and back one. If you think of the stairs as notes in a scale, you have performed a sequence.

Here are a couple of sequence patterns for an A Major scale, starting with the 2nd finger on the 6th string (see page 48). Use down-up picking.

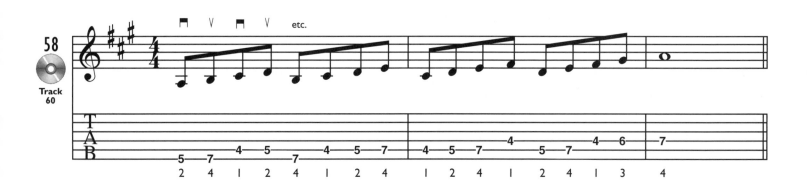

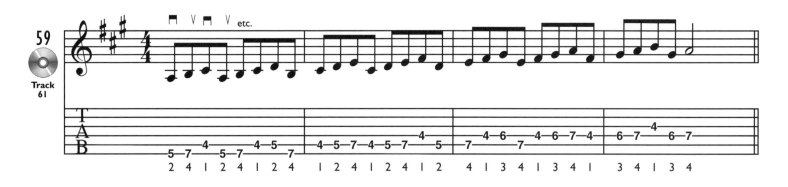

FLYING AROUND—REPETITION

Once you have begun with a sequence, you will want to try different ideas to create the body of your solo. One important concept for building a coherent solo is *repetition*. Repetition can help add a sense of structure to your solo and help it sound organized—like it's more than just a bunch of unrelated notes. Take a small idea and repeat it as the chords change. You will hear the character of the idea change as the harmony moves beneath it.

Here is a repeated idea shown with the chord progression from example 57. Notice the sense of tension and resolution as the chords change under the repeated melody.

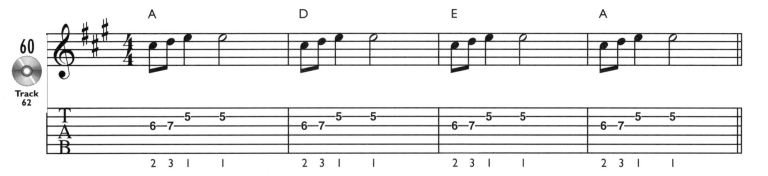

LANDING THE PLANE—EMPHASIZE THE TONIC

One way to create a sense of resolution in a solo, or even make a small *phrase* (complete musical thought) within a solo, is to bring it to rest on the tonic (1st degree of the major scale of the key). In this case, that would be an A note. Play a short passage that ends on 1 and allow the note to last for a few beats. This allows some "breathing space" before the start of your next idea.

Here are two phrases that illustrate the technique of coming to rest on the 1st degree. They are shown with the chord progression from example 57.

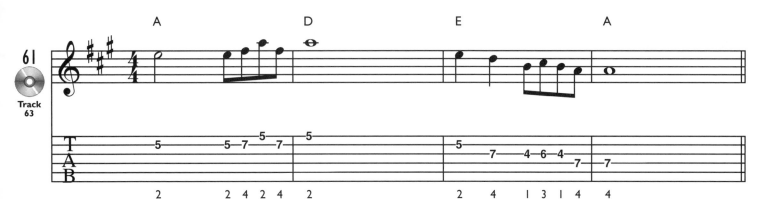

As you continue through this three-book method, you will learn lots of new techniques, scales and chords but these basic improvisational concepts will always hold true. Apply them every chance you get!

CHAPTER 6

The Blues

The blues is so much a part of American music that its influence is felt in nearly every style. Far more than just the feeling of good times that done gone bad,

> **the blues is:**
> • **A musical style**
> • **A form of poetry**
> • **A type of scale**
> • **An additude**
> • **A specific musical form and chord progression**
> • **An incurable, infectious human condition**
> **that is both miserable and joyful at the same time**

LESSON 1: THE TWELVE-BAR BLUES

THE FORM

The *twelve-bar blues* is one of the most basic song *forms*. The form is the organization or structure of a piece. The twelve-bar blues derives its name from the number of measures (also called bars) in the form. Below is a common version of the twelve-bar blues in the key of A. Included are chord symbols and Roman numerals indicating the analysis of the harmony. Try it with either simple downstrokes or a strum pattern from page 31.

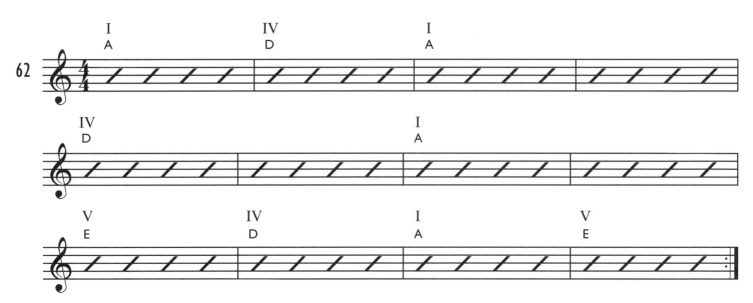

LESSON 2: MEMORIZING THE TWELVE-BAR BLUES

WHY MEMORIZE IT? TO JAM, OF COURSE

There may be times when you want to play with other people who don't know the same songs you do. The twelve-bar blues is widely known by musicians at all levels of experience. A working knowledge of how to play through the progression, as well as improvising on it, can give you an "ace up your sleeve" in those difficult situations when you can't decide what to "jam" on.

BLUES POETRY

The twelve-bar blues is organized in three lines of four measures each. This mirrors the poetic form of many blues lyrics. A common form of blues lyric consists of a statement (line 1), a repetition of the statement (line 2) and a sort of "clincher" (line 3). Check out these common blues verses:

> *My baby just left me, and man I feel so bad*
> *My baby just left me, and man I feel so bad*
> *Since my baby left me, I lost everything I had*
>
> *I'd rather drink muddy water, sleep in a hollow log*
> *I'd rather drink muddy water, sleep in a hollow log*
> *Than stay in this city, treated like a dirty dog*

PLAY BY NUMBERS

You may have noticed that the blues contains the three primary chords discussed on page 59. These are the I, IV and V (one, four and five) chords. In the key of A, these would be:

$$I = A \qquad IV = D \qquad V = E$$

Try to memorize the progression using these numbers. That way, you will learn its structure without being limited to the key of A. Soon, you will be able play the blues in any key, as long as you know what the I, IV and V chords are for that key. To make it easier, memorize one line at a time.

PLAY IT IN YOUR SLEEP

To get the most out of learning the blues, try to memorize the progression. Be able to play it over and over without losing your place in the form. This will make it much easier to jam with other players. You will be able to enjoy the musical interaction of the moment without worrying about whether you brought your music or whether you are on bar 10 or bar 6.

In addition, you should know that there are many, many variations possible on the twelve-bar blues form. Some have more chords, some have fewer, some have different chords substituted for the common ones. By burning a specific, basic version of the pattern into your brain through repetition and study, you will have an easier time compensating for slight variations from song to song.

THE ALMIGHTY SHUFFLE—SWING EIGHTHS

While the blues progression can be played with any rhythm (from bluegrass to punk to reggae and beyond), the *swing shuffle* is the most recognizable blues rhythm. It is very easy to play and has a propulsive, rocking sound that feels good at any speed.

The first step to learning the shuffle is to learn a new counting rhythm. Until now, you have been counting eighth notes in a steady, even beat like this:

These are known in musical lingo as *straight eighths* because each eighth note is the same length. *Swing eighths* are heard in jazz, blues, rockabilly and folk music. In swing eighths, the on-beat is given longer emphasis while the off-beat ("&") is made shorter.

The best way to understand the swing rhythm is to relate the eighths to *eighth-note triplets*. These are groups of three eighth notes that are played in the time of two (one beat). To get the feel, try saying this aloud to a steady beat: "trip-pul-let, trip-pul-let."

In swing eighths, the first two notes of the triplet are tied together.

Swing eighths are usually designated in music in one of two ways:

In this method, we use the latter of the two, *Swing 8ths*. Often, out there in the real world, there is no indication given at all; blues and jazz players just automatically swing the eighths. *And the real kicker is that swing eighths look just like straight eighths!*

PLAYING THE SHUFFLE ON AN A CHORD

One of the most popular blues rhythm figures is called *the shuffle*. We use the swing eighth rhythm with two-note chords. The lower note is the root. The higher note alternates between an interval of a perfect 5th and a major 6th above the root. Here is the way to play it for an A chord:

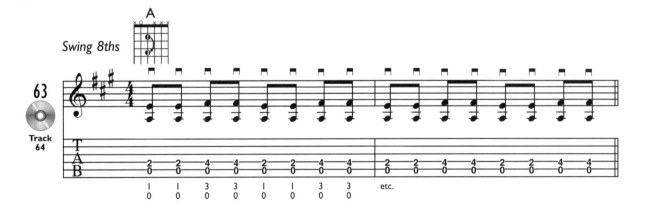

SHUFFLING ON D AND E CHORDS

Here is the shuffle for the D and E chords in a twelve-bar blues. Notice that all you have to do is move the 4th- and 5th-string pattern for the A shuffle on page 64 to the 3rd and 4th strings for the D chord and then down to the 5th and 6th strings for the E chord.

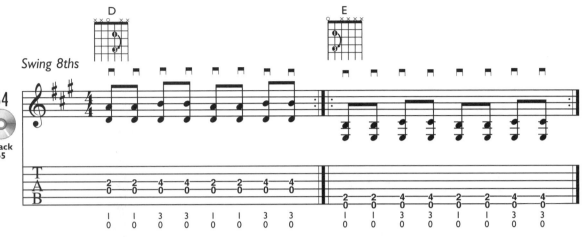

SHUFFLIN' THROUGH THE BLUES IN A

LESSON 4: THE MINOR PENTATONIC SCALE

Many blues melodies and solos use the notes of the *minor pentatonic scale*. Unlike the major scale (page 46), which has seven different notes, the minor pentatonic scale has only five different notes (*penta* is the Greek word meaning "five"). Pentatonic scales are very common in folk and traditional music from many cultures around the world.

THE MINOR PENTATONIC SCALE IN A

The same five notes are repeated as needed to cross all six strings of the guitar.

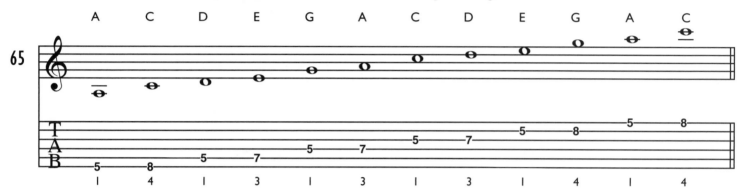

Below is a great fingering for the scale, shown in a single diagram. Play it one note at a time, starting on the 6th string and ascending to the 1st, then descending.

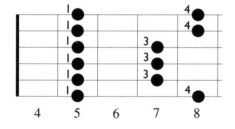

Here are the notes used in the A Minor Pentatonic scale fingering.

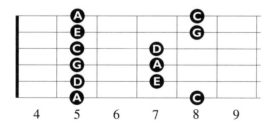

SCALE DEGREES

The minor pentatonic scale can be shown in scale degrees (page 46) just like the major scale. The scale degrees allow you to compare the minor pentatonic scale with the major scale to see which notes are the same and which are different.

A MAJOR SCALE:	1	2	3	4	5	6	7
	A	B	C#	D	E	F#	G#
A MINOR PENTATONIC SCALE:	1		♭3*	4	5		♭7*
	A		C	D	E		G

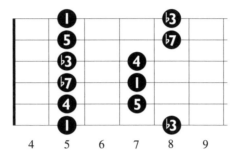

* The flat before the 3 (♭3) and 7(♭7) tells us that these notes are one half step lower than 3 and 7 in the major scale.

The minor pentatonic scale does not use a 2nd or 6th degree. In addition, the 3rd and 7th degrees are one half step lower than they are in the major scale. Musicians refer to these as "flat three" (♭3) and "flat seven" (♭7). These are the famous *blue notes* of the scale.

BLUE NOTES

When a scale has a lowered 3rd degree (flat three), it is said to be a *minor scale*. The cool thing about the blues is that, while the chords are often major, the melody is often minor. This creates a funky, slightly dissonant clash between the chords and the blue notes in the melody and gives the blues its melancholy, expressive sound.

In the old African scales that lie at the core of the blues, the blue notes were actually played somewhere between the blue note and the regular scale note (for example, between C and C# in the key of A). Guitarists often approximate this sound by *bending* the string (actually pushing the string up toward the ceiling or pulling it down toward the floor as explained on page 69) to the blue note, or by *sliding* (gliding along the string to make a sliding sound) from one fret to another. You'll learn these and other techniques later in this method.

LESSON 5: BEGINNING BLUES IMPROVISATION

EXPERIMENTING WITH THE SCALE

The first step to improvising a blues solo is learning to get around in the minor pentatonic scale. Try to make up melodies that use the minor pentatonic scale. Go up a few notes, go down a few notes. Play long and short notes. Skip around. Don't worry about whether it's "right" or "wrong"—just try to stick to the notes in the scale. Above all, have fun and aim for clean, clear tones. Let your ear be your guide. With patience, time and experimentation, you will develop many ideas that you can use in improvising on the blues.

GET IN YOUR LICKS

A *lick* is a small idea or figure that can be used as a building block for a solo. A lick can be repeated, altered or strung together with other licks. This lesson will show you a few ideas for licks that you can incorporate into your improvisations.

EMPHASIZING THE TONAL CENTER

As discussed on page 61, a great way to give a sense of melody and structure to a solo is to emphasize the tonic (1st scale degree). This note is also known as the *tonal center*. Blues players like B.B. King and Eric Clapton often play long, rich notes on the tonal center.

Here are some licks to try. They can be used at any point in the blues chord progression.

LESSON 6: BENDING

Guitarists often imitate the African vocal sound that is the basis of the blues by *bending* the strings. When we push or pull on a string with the left hand to actually change its shape, we create a smooth, gliding sound that few other instruments can achieve. This allows us to move smoothly into important notes, such as the blue notes discussed on page 67.

Here are a few tips to help you with your bending technique:

1. Try to use the 3rd finger to perform most of your bends, lining up the 1st and 2nd fingers behind it for support. This will get you the maximum leverage (and require the least strength).

2. If necessary, change your hand position so that your thumb hooks over the top of the neck slightly. Use your whole wrist and hand in a "cranking" or "choking" motion to bend the string.

THE $\flat$5 BLUE NOTE

Hidden inconspicuously between the 4th and 5th degrees of the minor pentatonic scale, the $\flat$5 is perhaps the most effective blue note. It adds an unmistakeably "bluesy" quality to any melody. It is a great note to approach with a bend. Try it in the key of A. Here's how:

1. Find the 4th degree of an A Minor Pentatonic scale (D) on the 7th fret of the 3rd string. Play this with your 3rd finger and line up your 1st and 2nd fingers behind it.

2. Add your 4th finger to the 8th fret and listen to the sound of that note, E$\flat$, the $\flat$5. You will need to have this sound in your ear to perfect the bend in the next step.

3. Using your thumb and wrist for leverage, play the note D, then push the string up towards the ceiling. Keep the pressure on the string and listen to the note glide up. Stop pushing when it sounds like the note you played in step 2. This is called a *half-step bend*, because we are bending up to a note one half step higher.

In written music, this is indicated with a *grace* note (a small note) and an arrow pointing up with a "½" above it, to indicate a half-step bend.

Try example 67 using the bend to $\flat$5. This lick can be repeated all the way through the blues progression. Try it and see how the character of the lick changes depending on which chord is being played. If the strings on your guitar simply won't bend, you can approximate the effect by sliding your finger from the 7th to the 8th fret, keeping the pressure on the string as you go. Don't pluck the second note in the slide.

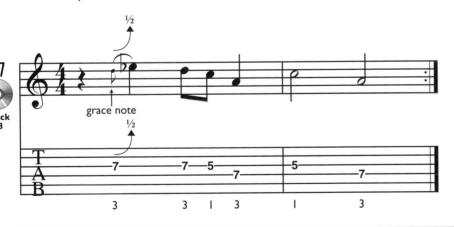

67
Track 68

> If you're having trouble bending notes on your acoustic guitar, do not despair. Steel-string acoustics have thicker strings with higher tension than electric guitars. If you're playing a nylon-string guitar (classical guitar), you may find it easy to bend but you may not hear much change in pitch. Nylon strings are very flexible and harder to bend to new notes. Be patient and keep trying!

Up to this point, you have been playing triads, which are three-note chords. To add more harmonic color to the blues (as well as other styles), you can use 7th chords. A 7th chord consists of a triad (root, 3rd and 5th) with the interval of a major or minor 7th added above the root. There are several different types of 7th chords, built with different combinations of intervals.

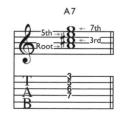

The most common 7th chord in the blues is the *dominant 7th* chord. This is a major triad (such as I, IV or V) with a minor 7th interval added above the root. Remember that a minor 7th interval is ten half steps above the root—or, one whole step below the octave (see pages 50 and 55). The fingering shown here is a bit tough to play but shows the chord tones in a logical, easy to understand way. Below, you'll learn some easy fingerings.

Following are some fingerings for dominant 7th chords you can use in the blues. Note that a dominant 7th chord is indicated with the addition of a "7" to the chord name, such as A7 or D7. Other types of 7th chords will carry different designations. It is also very common to hear 7th chords simply referred to as "7" chords ("seven" chords). This is because there is no "th" in the actual chord names.

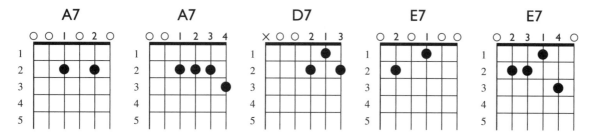

Try these fingerings with the twelve-bar blues. Use downstrokes or make up a strum rhythm.

7 CHORD BLUES

Track 69

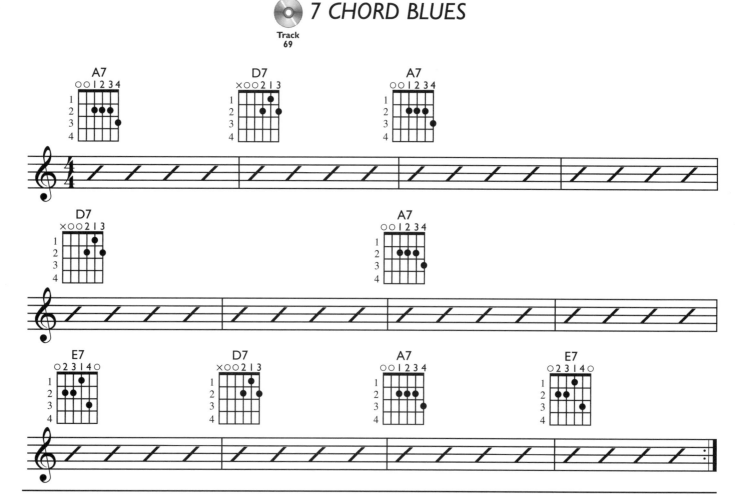

Here are some more fingerings for dominant 7 chords:

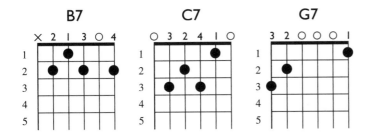

You can use these chords to play the blues in a different key. This is called *transposing* (see page 78). To transpose the blues to the key of E, ask yourself, "What are the I, IV and V chords in the key of E?" (See pages 58 and 59 to review the subject of diatonic harmony.) The correct answers are at the bottom of the page.

$$\overline{\text{I}} \qquad \overline{\text{IV}} \qquad \overline{\text{V}}$$

Try playing the twelve-bar blues in E, using dominant 7 chords.

 THE TWELVE-BAR BLUES IN E

Track 70

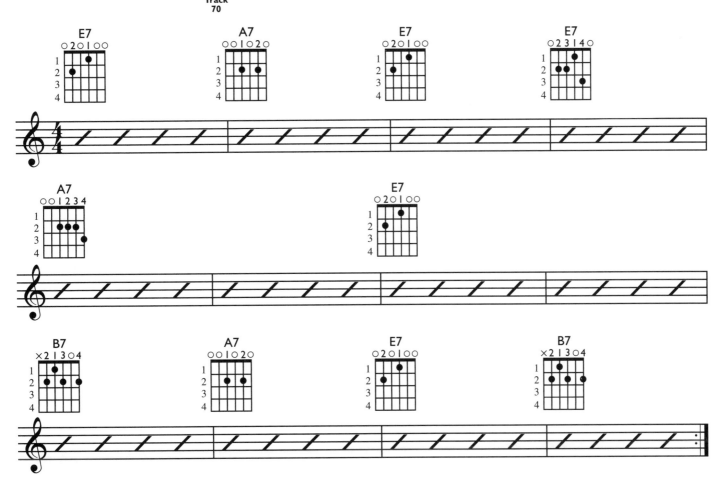

Now, try playing a twelve-bar blues in G using dominant 7 chords. The chords will be G7 (I, shown above), C7 (IV, shown above) and D7 (V, shown on page 70).

Answers:

The I chord is E, the IV chord is A and the V chord is B.

The blues can be played using minor chords, giving it a dark, emotional sound. One of the most famous minor blues songs is B.B. King's *The Thrill Is Gone*. Try playing the blues using triads in the key of A Minor. (See page 28 to review minor chord fingerings.)

A MINOR BLUES

Track 71

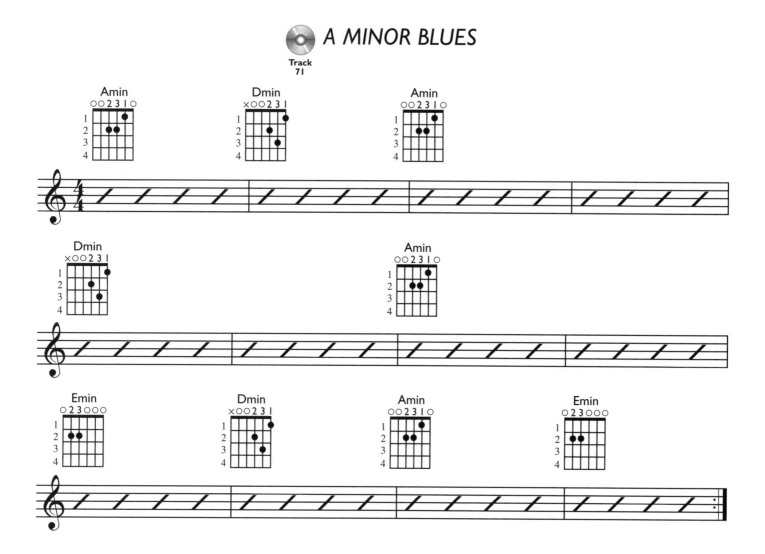

BLUES SOLOING IN A MINOR KEY

One advantage of learning the minor pentatonic scale is that it works for both major and minor blues songs. To improvise over the twelve-bar blues in A Minor, simply use the same A Minor Pentatonic scale you learned on page 66.

Minor 7th chords (min7) are similar to dominant 7ths, except that the triad is minor. Here is an A Minor 7 chord:

The fingering shown here shows the notes of the chord in an easy-to-understand manner, but is somewhat impractical to play. Below are some easy fingerings for minor 7th chords. You will find that they have more color than simple minor chords, and that they can be easily substituted for them. In other words, when you see Amin in the music, you can choose to play Amin7 instead.

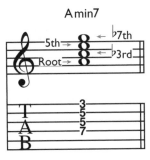

Here are some easy minor 7 fingerings:

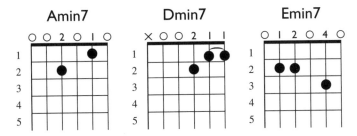

Try using minor seventh chords with the twelve-bar blues progression.

MINOR 7 BLUES

Track 72

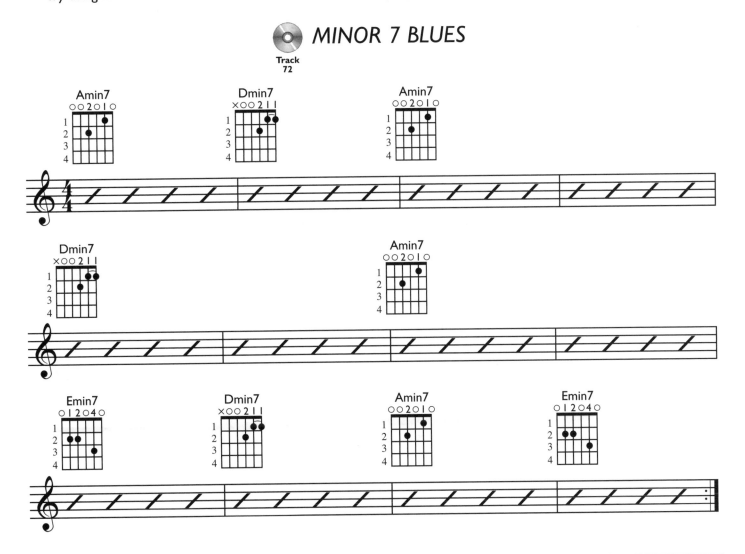

CHAPTER 7

New Techniques

LESSON 1: SWITCHING CHORDS MID-MEASURE

If you have looked at sheet music or songbooks, you have probably noticed that chords don't always change on the first beat of the measure. Even in this book, there have been examples of chords switching on beat 3 (for example, *Heavy Fog* on page 28). If you are doing simple downstrokes or a simple strum, it is fairly easy to adjust. However, if you are playing the syncopated strum from page 36, it can be tricky to know how to switch. Here are three techniques you can try:

TECHNIQUE #1: MIXING STRUMS

The easiest thing to do is to switch to a simpler strum when the chord switching becomes more complex.

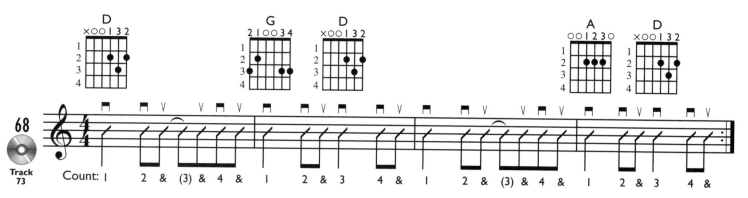

TECHNIQUE #2: SWITCHING ON THE "&" OF BEAT 2

This will cause your chord switch to come a half-beat early. It gives the chord change a funky sense of anticipation.

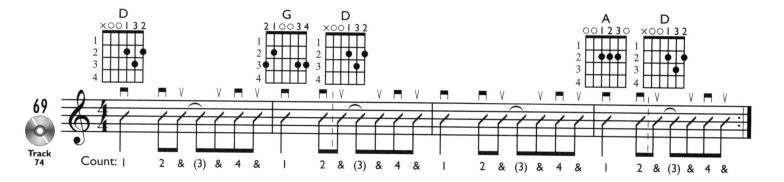

TECHNIQUE #3: SWITCHING ON THE "&" OF BEAT 3

This will cause your chords to change half-a-beat late. This is also funky but in a different way.
Try mixing Techniques #1, #2 and #3 together in the same song.

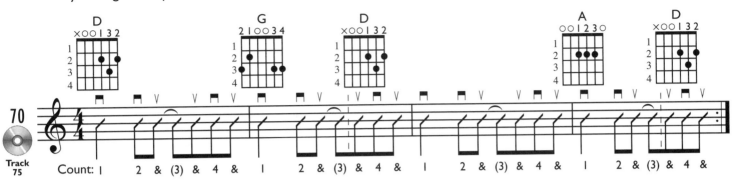

LESSON 2: SPLIT STRUMMING

Many solo acoustic artists use special strumming techniques to create the impression of multiple guitars. One technique is to mentally "split" the strings of the guitar into two groups:

The *bass* group:	Strings 4, 5, 6
The *treble* group:	Strings 1, 2, 3

You can then accent a different group on different parts of the strum. Sometimes, accent the bass group. Then suprise the listener by accenting the treble group instead. This will impart a jangly, dynamic sound to your playing. This technique is heard in the playing of Neil Young, Ani DiFranco, Michael Hedges, Joni Mitchell and many others.

Enjoy playing *I Know How it Feels*, which is in the style of Tom Petty's *You Don't Know How it Feels*. Hit the bass group on beats 1 and 2, then the treble group on beats 3 and 4.

I KNOW HOW IT FEELS

Track 76

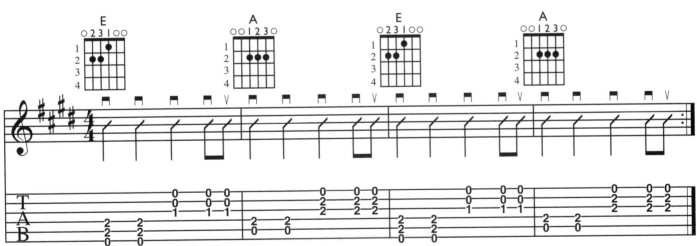

> **SECRETS OF THE MASTERS:**
> **Don't try to be too precise with this style! Play it loose and relaxed.**

Another technique that can give the impression of multiple instruments is the *mute stroke*. A mute stroke is a strum (usually a downstroke) that mutes the strings as the pick hits them, creating a percussive sound. Mute strokes can be mixed in with normal downstrokes and upstrokes in a strum pattern.

STEP #1: GETTING THE IDEA

First, place the heel of your right hand (the fleshy part on the "pinky" side) across the strings somewhere between the sound hole and the bridge.

Second, move the pick across the strings while the heel of your hand is muting them. You should hear no notes, just a percussive, clicky, raspy kind of sound.

✕   This symbol is generally reserved for percussive, unpitched sounds. The mute stroke is not completely unpitched, but this is still an effective way to notate this kind of sound.

STEP #2: THE MUTE STROKE

Now try to make the same sound in a normal downstroke. Start with your hand off the guitar as if you were going to strum down. Then as you contact the strings, mute them with the heel of your hand. This may take some practice but don't give up!

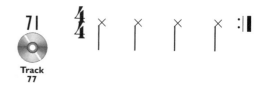

STEP #3: THE COMBINATION MOVE

Once you've got the downstroke, finger a G chord with your left hand. Play a mute stroke down, then sound the G chord on the upstroke.

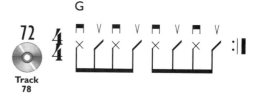

PUTTING IT ALL TOGETHER

Try the following strum pattern with mute strokes. When played properly, it will have the sound of a *backbeat* (stressed notes on beats 2 and 4) and the percussive effect will sound much like a rock drummer.

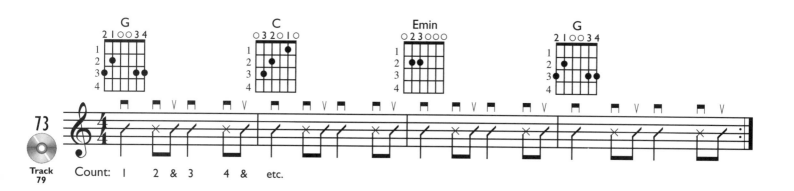

This strum pattern has been very popular with guitarist-singers since the folk revival of the early 1960s. It has been heavily used by Bob Dylan and Indigo Girls.

The strum pattern is based on the country/bluegrass strum but is not as rigid sounding. It combines the "boom-chick" effect with the jangle of the syncopated strum. Before you try this one, review the country/bluegrass strums on page 32.

Try this pattern with the bluegrass G chord (page 29).

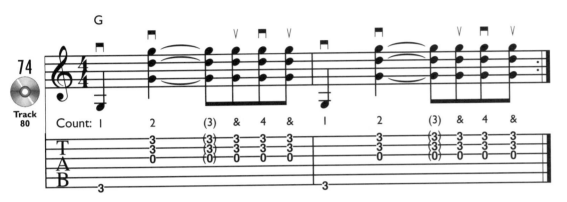

This strum is very versatile in that it can be played fast or slow, with a straight or swing beat. At first, try it slowly with swing (to review eighths check out page 64). Then, as you get the hang of it, try speeding it up with a straight beat.

Try this chord progression with the "other" folk strum.

FLUTTERING IN THE BREEZE

Track 81

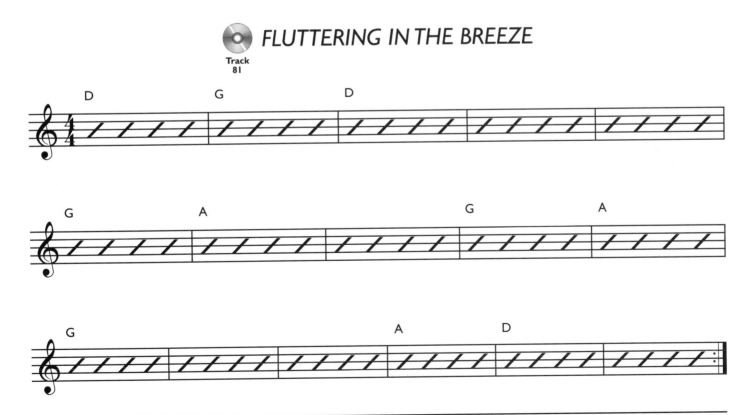

LESSON 5: TRANSPOSITION

Transposing means changing the key of a song. You have already tried this by learning the same twelve-bar blues progression in both A and E (pages 62 and 71).

WHY TRANSPOSE?

The most common reason for transposing a song to a new key is to better fit the vocal range of a singer. For example, imagine a song in the key of E. If the key of E is too high, you could transpose down to D, or even C. Another reason to transpose is to make a song easier to play on the guitar.

THE SUBSTITUTION METHOD

This method of transposition is the easiest to learn but not the most efficient. First, consider this chord progression in the key of G. Play it with the syncopated strum.

TRANSPOSING TO THE KEY OF D

First, you must know how far the new key is from the original key. The key of D is a perfect 5th (seven half steps) higher than the key of G. To transpose the song, substitute each of the original chords with the chord a perfect 5th higher.

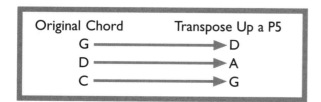

Here is the progression from example 75 transposed up a perfect 5th to D:

TRANSPOSING TO THE KEY OF A

Try using this method yourself. The answers are at the end of the lesson on page 79.

1. How far above G is A?
2. What is the new chord progression?

Transpose example 75 to the key of A (write in your answers):

THE CHORD ANALYSIS METHOD

This method takes more practice and thought at first but eventually, you will be able to transpose songs without having to write the new chords.

Here is your example progression, in the key of D.

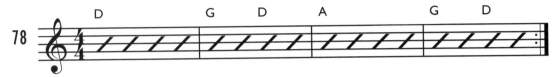

TRANSPOSING TO THE KEY OF G

First, analyze the chord progression by chord numbers. Think of the diatonic harmony in D and determine the position of each chord in the key.

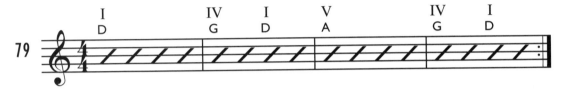

Now you are ready to transpose to any key. Try the key of G.

KEY OF G: I = G   IV = C   V = D

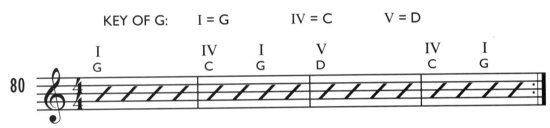

TRANSPOSING TO THE KEY OF A

Try this one yourself. (See the answer at the bottom of this page)

KEY OF A: I =   IV =   V =

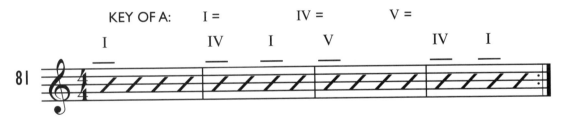

ANSWERS TO EXAMPLE 77:

1. The key of A is one whole step higher than the key of G.

ANSWERS TO EXAMPLE 81:

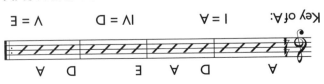

A power chord (first covered on page 53) is a two-note chord that consists of a root and a 5th. Because the power chord has no 3rd, it can be used in place of either a major or a minor chord.

The power chord is a movable shape (it can be played on any fret) that is usually played on the lower strings of the guitar. It is very common in rock, punk, heavy metal and blues guitar. Power chords are especially popular among electric guitar players because of the way they resonate when played with lots of distortion. Many acoustic players who plug in like them for the same reason.

The power chord shape is easy to remember. Play the root (the lower note) with your 1st finger. The 5th (the upper note) is on the next string, two frets up, and is played with the 3rd finger. Try these:

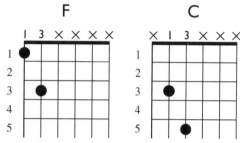

Here is a song using power chords. Play all the eighth notes with downstrokes.

RAGE AGAINST THE GUMBALL MACHINE

Track 82

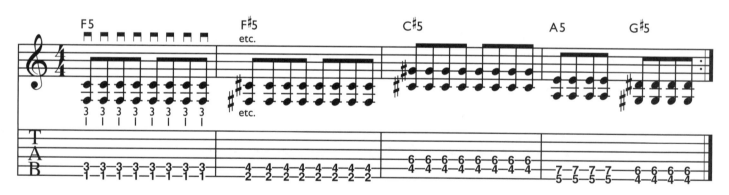

PALM MUTING

Palm muting is commonly used by rock guitarists. It is very similar to the mute stroke on page 76. Use the heel of your right hand to lightly touch the strings just to the left of the bridge.

This effect will "tighten up" the sound of the chords and make them more percussive. If you move too close to the sound hole, you will kill the notes completely. Experiment to find the best position. This effect is also great for the blues shuffle you learned on page 64. Try *Rage Against the Gumball Machine* on page 80 with *palm muting*, and prepare to fend off the groupies!

THREE-NOTE POWER CHORDS

For a thicker, chunkier power chord, you can add an octave above the root. Below are some examples. Try these with *Rage Against the Gumball Machine*.

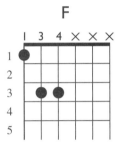

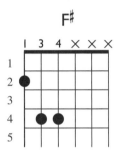

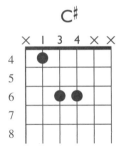

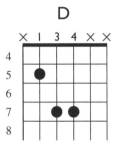

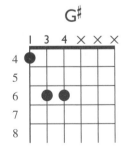

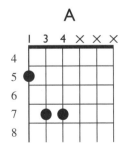

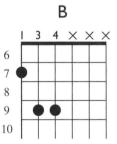

Congratulations! You've made it this far and now you're ready for your biggest challenge yet...

LESSON 7: BARRE CHORDS

WHAT IS A BARRE CHORD?

A *barre chord* is a chord form that uses no open strings. It can be moved up or down the neck to play any chord.

BARRE CHORDS WITH THE ROOT ON THE 6TH STRING

This barre chord form is also known as the *E-form* barre chord because it is based on the shape of the open E chord (page 15). Simply finger an E chord using the 2nd, 3rd and 4th fingers and leave the 1st finger free to hold the barre. The root is on the 6th string. This barre chord shape is available in both major and minor forms. The minor form is based on the open E Minor chord but is refingered to leave the 1st finger free to barre.

F Major

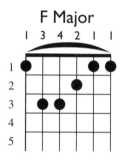

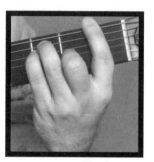

F Minor

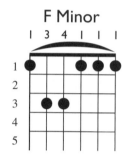

= Barre

BARRE CHORDS WITH THE ROOT ON THE 5TH STRING

These are also known as *A-form* barre chords. Simply finger an A chord using the 2nd, 3rd and 4th fingers and leave the 1st finger free to hold the barre. The root is on the 5th string. Here are the major and minor forms. The minor form is based on the open A Minor form but is refingered to leave the 1st finger free to barre.

B♭ Major

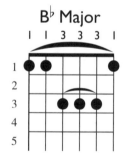

B♭ Minor

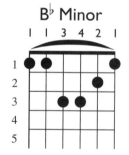

Try these chord progressions with barre chords. Fingerings are provided. Make sure to watch the fret numbers!

PASSING THE BARRE

Track 83

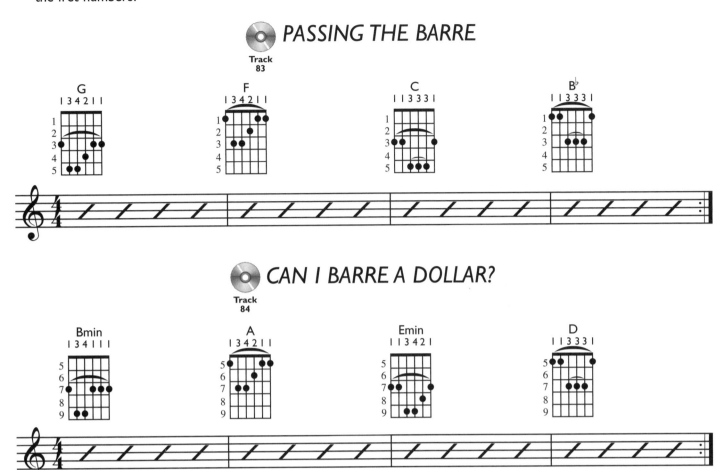

CAN I BARRE A DOLLAR?

Track 84

SECRETS OF THE MASTERS: TIPS FOR LEARNING BARRE CHORDS

1. **Start with a mini-barre.** (No—not the refrigerator in your hotel room.) Master a two-string barre on an easy fret to barre, such as the 5th fret, then a three-string barre, and so on.

2. **Be picky and efficient.** Don't work on having a beautiful barre sound on a string if another finger is playing above the barre on that string! For example, in an E-form barre, only the 1st, 2nd and 6th strings really need an excellent barre. Other fingers are covering the other strings.

3. **Use leverage.** Bring your left elbow in slightly toward your body, thus moving your 1st finger further into the strings without actually pressing any harder.

4. **Be Patient!** Don't worry if you don't get these right away. Work on them a little every day. Try to get each note in the chord to ring clearly. If you have problems in the first few frets, where the string tension is higher, try moving up to the 5th, 6th or 7th frets.

5. **Gravity is your friend!** Try not to twist your left hand into wild contortions and squeeze all of the blood out of your fingers. Instead, let your left wrist and elbow hang down in a relaxed way. Feel the pull of gravity and let it help your 1st finger "hang" on the fret.

Hammer-ons and *pull-offs* are special techniques that add fluidity and speed to melodic playing. Both techniques allow you to play multiple notes on one string with only one stroke of the pick. In musical terms, this is called a *slur* and is denoted by a curved line connecting notes of different pitches. Be careful not to confuse this with a tie which connects notes of the same pitch.

HAMMER-ON EXERCISE

To play a hammer-on, pick a note and bring a higher-numbered finger down on a higher fret quickly and firmly. You should hear the note change without having to pick again. Here is an exercise for working on hammer-ons with each finger. Try this on each string at different places on the neck.

H = Hammer-on

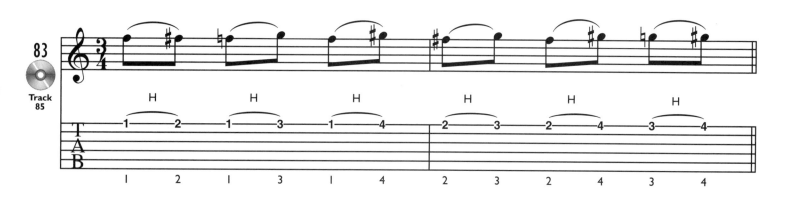

PULL-OFF EXERCISE

To play a pull-off, place two fingers down on two frets and play the note on the higher fret. Then, pull the higher-numbered finger away from the higher fret, making the lower-fret note sound without picking. When pulling-off, don't just lift up your finger; instead, give it a little "snap" by pulling your finger in towards your palm. Example 84 is an exercise for pull-offs. Try it on each string at different places on the neck.

P = Pull-off

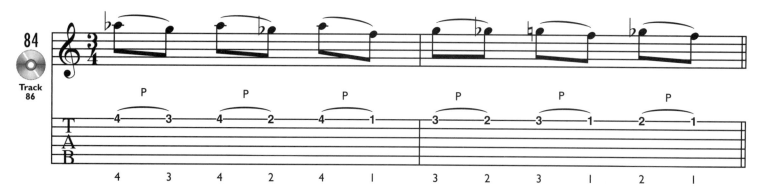

1st and 2nd Endings Review

Often, when we repeat a section, we play the last part of it differently. In the written music, this is shown with *1st* and *2nd endings*.

The first time through, play the music under the bracket with a "1" (the *1st ending*). The second time, skip the 1st ending and play the music under the bracket marked "2" (the *2nd ending*).

Blue Noodles on an E Chord uses hammer-ons and pull-offs surrounding the shape of an E chord. Go slowly and aim for clean notes. Try to make the slurred notes sound at the same volume as the picked notes. Also, try to incorporate slurs into your improvisations.

 BLUE NOODLES ON AN E CHORD

Track 87

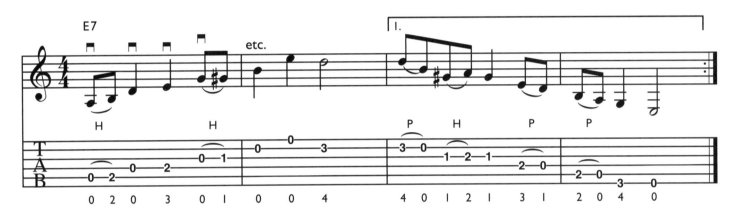

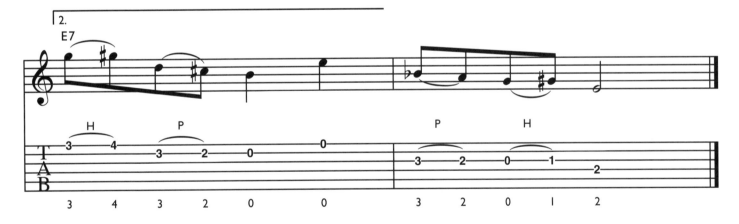

A fun way to spice up your country/bluegrass-style strumming (page 32) is to use short melodies in the bass to connect the roots of the chords. This is called *walking the bass*. Adding simple walks to your bass line helps "lead" the listener's ear to the next chord. This is like using a turn signal on a car to show the person following you where you're going. Here are a few simple walks for the key of G.

WALKING FROM A G CHORD TO A C CHORD

Adding a walk to a chord progression is very simple if you count! The walk in example 85 takes up the last two beats of the second measure. Before you try this, review your chord fingerings and strums from page 32.

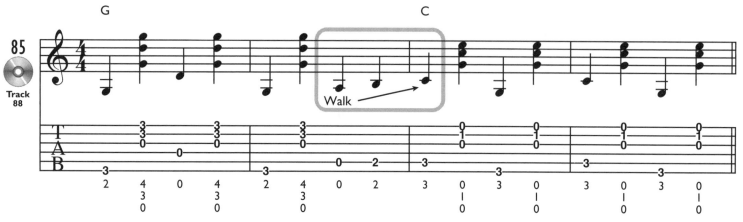

WALKING FROM A G CHORD TO A D CHORD

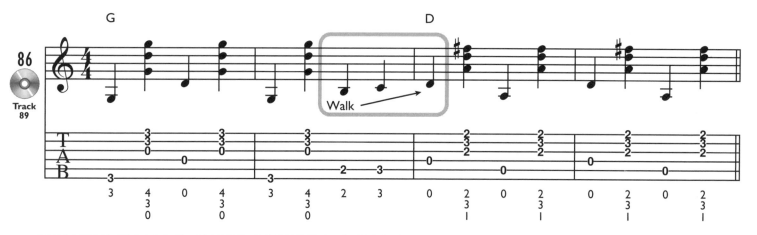

WALKING FROM A D CHORD BACK TO A G CHORD

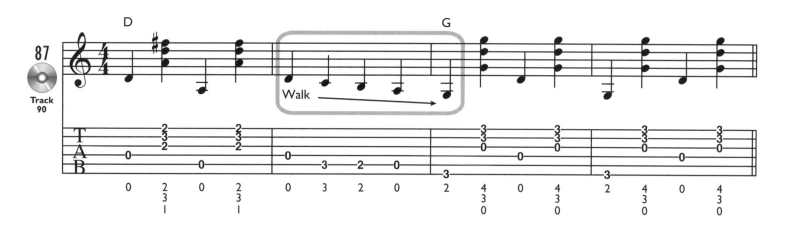

This is the chord progression from an old traditional Appalachian tune called *Free Little Bird*. It allows you to try out your bass walks. Try making up some walks of your own, too. Just make sure you have the correct number of beats in every measure.

FREE LITTLE BIRD

Track 91

CHAPTER 8

Musical Expression and Arranging

LESSON 1: PHRASING AND DYNAMICS

EXPRESSION

Music is not just about keeping time and playing the right notes or chords. In order for music to have an emotional effect, it needs a sense of *expression*. Two very important elements of musical expression are *phrasing* and *dynamics*.

PHRASING

Phrasing is the way that touch, volume and tempo are used to imply a sense of direction, movement and rest in a piece of music. If notes are like words, then phrasing is the way that the words are made to sound like sentences, or complete thoughts.

PHRASING MARKINGS

Written music uses a large number of markings and terms to communicate phrasing and expression to the performer. Many of these terms are Italian. A quick tour of some commonly used terms should give you some ideas for your own music. First, the *phrase mark* is a curved line that loosely connects an entire passage of music. It can be confused with a slur or a tie, but the phrase mark is usually shown above the staff and may have slurs or ties beneath it.

Phrase Mark

OTHER PHRASING AND EXPRESSION TERMS		
TERM	DEFINITION	MARKING
Legato	Notes are to be played in a smooth, connected fashion.	The word "Legato" marked above the music.
Staccato	Short, detached, unconnected notes.	The word "*Staccato*" marked above the music, or small dots above or below individual note heads.
Accent	A note played louder than the surrounding notes.	This sign $>$ above or below the note head.

DYNAMICS

Dynamics define how loud or soft the notes or passages of music will sound. Dynamic expression and contrast is very important to imparting a sense of emotion in a piece of music.

LOUD			SOFT		
Mark	**Term**	**Definition**	**Mark**	**Term**	**Definition**
mf	Mezzo Forte	Medium Loud	*mp*	Mezzo Piano	Medium soft
f	Forte	Loud	*p*	Piano	Soft
ff	Fortissimo	Very Loud	*pp*	Pianissimo	Very soft
fff	Fortississimo	Very, very loud	*ppp*	Pianississimo	Very, very soft
———<	Crescendo	Gradually becoming louder	>———	Decrescendo	Gradually becoming softer

THE DYNAMIC SCALE

Arranged from softest to loudest, the dynamic markings look like this:

Softest   Loudest

THE "ARCH"

Many times a phrase or an entire piece of music will lend itself to a dynamic "arch" that begins at a softer dynamic, climaxes at a louder dynamic, then returns to a softer level. This is especially true if the melody moves from low notes up to high notes, then back down. Look for opportunities to place this kind of expression in your music. Also look for spots where a "reverse arch" (loud to soft to loud) might work.

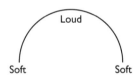

TIPS FOR EXPRESSIVE TECHNIQUE

It takes good control of the pick (or of your fingers) to bring out dynamics and phrasing with your right hand. Here are a few tips:

To play louder
Slightly tighten the grip on your pick. Do not pick "deeper" into the string, or try to use more muscle force. This makes a harsh tone.

To play softer
Slightly loosen the grip on your pick (but don't drop it!).

To play legato
Try to pick notes at the same time as you fret them. Make sure your pick doesn't touch a vibrating string before it's time to pluck again, cutting off the previous note.

To play staccato
You can use your pick to cut off the note by placing it back on the string, or use your left hand to cut off the note by lifting your finger(s) up slightly from the fret(s).

LESSON 2: CREATING AN ARRANGEMENT

An *arrangement* is the musical setting of a song or composition. In simple terms, the song is *what* you play, and the arrangement is *how* you play it. If you've ever heard the same song done by different performers, you have heard the effects of arranging.

LOOKING FOR THE CLUES

When you are trying to build an arrangement of a song or instrumental tune, there are clues within the composition that can give you ideas for the arrangement. The way you interpret these clues will help put your own personality into the arrangement.

LYRICAL CLUES

If the song has words, you can use these to help you build your arrangement concept. For example, if the song has a sad undertone, you might choose a slow tempo and an intimate fingerpicked background. On the other hand, very effective arrangements have been made by contrasting the mood of the lyrics with the mood of the music. Very troubled lyrics can be set to an energetic, dancing background.

MUSICAL FORM

The *musical form* of a piece includes how many sections there are, how long the phrases are, and the order of the sections. For example, you might choose to arrange the *verses* (the parts of the song that tell the story; the lyrics change each time) of a song one way, and give a different style or feel to the *chorus* (the part of the song that expresses the basic idea; it's a refrain wherein the lyrics are always the same).

PRACTICAL CONSIDERATIONS

You may choose to place the song in a new key to better fit your voice. You may also choose your strums, picking patterns and chord fingerings to fit your own playing level.

UNITY AND CONTRAST

Unity and *contrast* are two terms that are used to describe the delicate balance that holds a work of art together and makes it interesting.

> **Unity** is repetition, similarity, the recurrence of ideas.
> **Contrast** is variation, change, alteration or the addition of new ideas.

Here are examples of some key musical elements, and how the concepts of unity and contrast can be applied to them.

MUSICAL ELEMENT	UNITY	CONTRAST
Texture	Using the same strum pattern throughout a song or section of a song.	Mixing strum patterns or mixing melody and chord playing in a song.
Tempo	Maintaining a consistent tempo throughout a song.	Altering the tempo of a section or phrase.
Dynamics	Maintaining a consistent volume or range of volumes throughout a song or section of a song.	Changing the dynamics of different sections of a song or following a dynamic pattern that adds emotional intensity.

EXAMPLE ARRANGEMENT

Try playing *Song of the Elusive Beach Moose* and check out the arrangement tips that have been added for the guitar part.

STEP #1: Play the chord progression of this song using a simple strum such as the syncopated strum.

STEP #2: Try the song using the strums, textures and dynamics as indicated.

 # SONG OF THE ELUSIVE BEACH MOOSE

Track 92

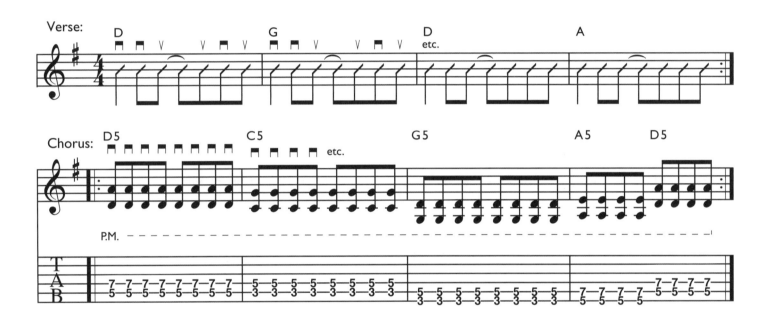

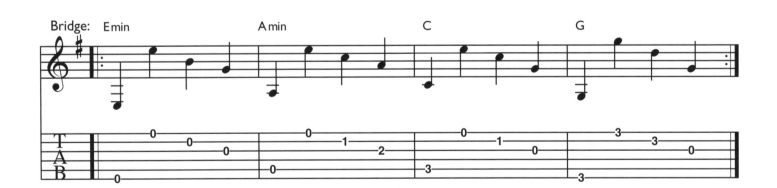

The form of the tune is as follows (each section is eight bars long):

Verse
Chorus
Verse
Chorus
Bridge
Verse
Chorus

APPENDIX

THE WONDERFUL CAPO, THE TERRIBLE CAPO

The capo is a device that clamps onto the guitar neck, fretting all six strings at whatever fret you choose. This fret then becomes like the nut of the guitar, allowing you to play all of your open chords in a higher key. There are many types and they all work (you pay for durability and convenience of design).

Try one and see how the capo can broaden the range of your instrument. The capo can become a bit of a crutch, however. Don't forget to try transposing to new keys without the capo (page 78).

TO FINGERPICK OR NOT TO FINGERPICK

Fingerpicking (discussed in Chapter 4) can be done with bare fingers, fingernails or with *fingerpicks*. Fingerpicks are made of plastic or metal and wrap around the fingers and/or thumb. Once you get used to them, they provide a clear, somewhat louder fingerpicked tone. Another advantage is that you don't have to worry about the condition of your nails because the fingerpicks give the same, consistent tone all the time.

Fingerpicks have many disadvantages, as well. They can compromise your technique, causing you to make special adjustments to your playing in order to get the pick "out of the way" for the next note. In addition, the consistent tone of fingerpicks does not allow for a variety of touches and sounds. Fingerpicks work very well for some players. On the other hand (no pun intended), playing without them affords the widest range of tonal colors, as well as the healthiest technique for the muscles of the hand and forearm. The problem of technical difficulties may be alleviated by checking out some of the new designs in fingerpicks.

One popular compromise is to use just a thumb pick. This allows the player to have clear, loud bass notes and a variety of colors in the touch of the fingers. Also, the thumb pick is popular with players who like to mix strumming and finger picking in the same song.

BUY A METRONOME!

A metronome is an adjustable mechanical device (either wind-up, battery-powered or digital) that generates a beat pulse for you to play along with. You can adjust the pulse from ridiculously slow to very fast. The speed is marked in "beats-per-minute." A metronome speed of 60 is the same as one beat-per-second. The simplest metronomes make a ticking sound, while the more involved ones will make drum sounds and even mark measures of beats for you.

When used regularly (and with a Zen-like patience), the metronome will help you play with a steady rhythm. The only practice technique that is as valuable is to play with another person who has good rhythm—this can be difficult to do on a daily basis.

Don't let the metronome drive you crazy! At first, it may appear to be speeding up and slowing down while you play. Listen carefully—it's probably you. Pick a consistent, slow tempo to work with for the first few days and try the metronome with one favorite song. See how many measures you can play before you and the metronome have a parting of the ways. Gradually increase your endurance before you increase the speed.

HELP WITH TUNING

One particularly tricky challenge for the beginning guitarist is keeping the instrument in tune. Tuning an instrument well takes a great deal of practice and experience. If you find that your chords are just not sounding quite right, consider investing in an electronic tuner.

Electronic tuners come in two basic designs: the guitar-only tuner and the chromatic tuner. The guitar-only tuner has settings for each of the open strings of the guitar. You just select the string, play it into the microphone on the tuner, and the tuner will show you if the note is sharp (too high), flat (too low) or in tune. An advantage of guitar tuners is that they are inexpensive. A disadvantage is that, if one of your strings is way off, the tuner will not know what note you are playing and may direct you to tune too high or low. A chromatic tuner listens to the note you are playing and tells you what note is the closest one, and whether you are sharp or flat from that note. Though a bit more expensive, these are more convenient for tuning a variety of instruments. Just make sure you know which string belongs to which note!

Don't rely completely on electronic tuners. After you've tuned with a tuner, make sure your strings are in tune with each other using the note-matching technique described on page 7. Play a few chords and see if they ring in tune. You may have to go back through the tuning process a few times before the instrument "settles" in tune.

FINGER STRENGTH BUILDERS

There are many gadgets and devices on the market that are designed to build finger strength. Usually these devices are meant to be squeezed with the fingers. While it is conceivable that such items could help build your strength to fret notes, be very careful. In general, devices that force you to squeeze against resistance are actually focusing on the wrong kinds of muscles. Guitar playing requires agility and accuracy more than brute strength. Agility and accuracy are built through practice and technique exercises. "Strength builders," however, can cause strain and inflammation to the muscles of the hand and forearm.

HOW TO PRACTICE

"HOME BASE" TECHNIQUE

It is important from the beginning to play with the best, most relaxed technique you can. Though you will see and learn many variations of technique, this will become the "home base" to which your body will always return. Building these good habits requires two elements:

1. TECHNIQUE EXERCISES

These allow you to concentrate on technique without worrying about keeping your place in the music.

2. MENTAL FOCUS IN PRACTICE

When you work on songs or new skills, be aware of your hand positions, body posture, rhythm and touch.

WHEN TO PRACTICE

When you are first beginning, or when you are learning new skills, it is best to practice often. Five to ten minutes here and there on a new skill will work much better than an hour every three or four days. If you're lucky enough to be able to practice at the same time every day, you will see great improvement. You will also notice that you develop a better ability to focus on guitar playing at that time. If it's not possible to practice at the same time every day, at least try to pick up the instrument for a few minutes every day, and then reinforce with longer sessions every couple of days.

WHAT TO PRACTICE

It is a great idea to have a small number of different "projects" going on in your practice sessions. This keeps you from getting bored or bogged down, and it helps you improve several skills at once. Pick two or three things to work on every day for a week, then adjust your plan for the next week. Some of these projects might include reading music, learning to improvise, playing a new melody or learning a new chord progression. Be sure to spend time on each project every time you play.

ORGANIZING A PRACTICE SESSION

Here's a sample 30-minute practice session you may want to try for a few weeks. If you have more or less time, adjust the time on each item.

1. Technical Exercises 5 minutes

These include finger exercises, counting and foot-tapping practice, warm-ups and scales.

2. Reading Music/Melody 10 minutes

Try reading lots of new material in order to keep your reading skills in shape. If you are not working on reading music, work on melody playing and improvising.

3. Playing Songs/Chords 10 minutes

Spend some time every day working on songs with chords. This may include working on new strums or fingerpicking patterns.

4. Reviewing Old Material 5 minutes

Always save a little time to go back and play songs you are already good at. This keeps them "tuned up" and ready to go for times when you want to play for relaxation or for other people.

INSPIRATIONAL LISTENING

WHAT TO LISTEN FOR

Every person who picks up an instrument has his or her own unique taste in music and inspiration for wanting to play. Now that you are delving deeper into the acoustic guitar, go back and listen to some of your favorite music and pay special attention to the guitarists. Notice the role of the guitar in the music—when it is playing and not playing. Pay attention to the touches and tones the player puts into the music. Is the player using a flatpick, or fingerpicking or something else altogether? Try to identify chords and rhythms that you are learning. You'll hear a lot of them!

In addition to listening to your old favorites with "new ears," try out some new music in styles you may have never heard or thought you'd like. Follow the suggestions of other guitarists or musicians. Remember not to limit yourself just to guitar! Every instrument has something exciting to offer the inquisitive musician.

Here are some acoustic guitarists to check out during the beginning phase of your development:

FOLK AND ROCK
Crosby, Stills, Nash and Young
Kurt Cobain (Nirvana)
Bob Dylan
Steve Earle
Melissa Etheridge
Jay Farrar (Son Volt and Uncle Tupelo)
Indigo Girls
Jewel
John Prine
Darius Rucker (Hootie & the Blowfish)
Jeff Tweedy (Wilco and Uncle Tupelo)

BLUES
John Lee Hooker
Mississippi John Hurt
Brownie McGhee

COUNTRY, BLUEGRASS AND OLD-TIME
The Carter Family
Johnny Cash
Lester Flatt (Flatt & Scruggs)
Cary Fridley (Freight Hoppers)
Nancy Griffith
Woody Guthrie

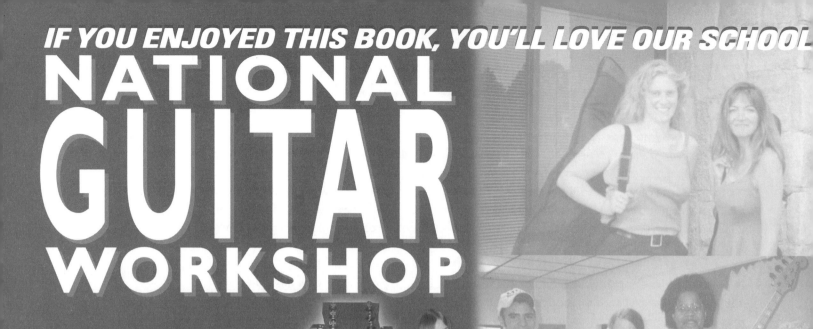